Published by:
POPULAR PRAKASHAN PVT. LTD.
301, Mahalaxmi Chambers
22, Bhulabhai Desai Road
Mumbai 400 026
for KALA GHODA ASSOCIATION

First Published 2016

ISBN - 978-81-7991-870-8
Master Code - 4429

Design and Concept: Brinda Miller, Heeral Akhaury and Nicole Mody
Book Design: Courtesy Spenta Multimedia Pvt. Ltd.
Photography: Shiresh R Karrale
Food Styling: Amrita Rana and Roxanne Bamboat
Sketches: Brinda Miller
Editor: Nicole Mody

Foreword by Vir Sanghvi

Printed in India by

SPENTA MULTIMEDIA PVT LTD
Peninsula Spenta, Mathuradas Mill Compound,
N. M. Joshi Marg, Lower Parel (W), Mumbai – 400 013.
Tel: +91-22-24811010 Fax: +91-22-24811021.
Website: www.spentamultimedia.com

Flavours OF KALA GHODA

RECIPES FROM THE ART DISTRICT

NICOLE MODY

Kala Ghoda Association | hindustantimes

FOREWORD

Cities have a complex relationship with food. I would wager that more people around the world have heard of the hamburger and the frankfurter than they have of Hamburg or Frankfurt. And often the relationship is based on legend rather than reality.

Take for instance Spaghetti Bolognese. The dish was created by Italian immigrants to Britain who bastardised the traditional Ragù pasta sauce of Bologna. Now, you even get Spaghetti Bolognese in Bologna – made for tourists in the bastardised way. Or take Chicken Kiev, the archetypal fancy restaurant dish that was on every menu in the middle of the last century. They made nothing like it in Kiev – it was Ukrainian immigrants to the US who created it. And yet, it is now touted in Kiev as the city's greatest dish!

India has had a mixed record. The British never credited us with the great dishes they stole from India during the Raj. Kedgeree may have been a country house staple in the days when Brits could still afford country houses but I doubt if the Earl of Grantham or any of the other residents of Downton Abbey realised that they were eating a tarted up Khichdi. (Apparently the Brits based it on a recipe for non-vegetarian khichdi they picked up in Bengal).

Or take Worcestershire sauce. It has got damn all to do with Worcester. The story goes that a retired Raj-era Brit went off to the firm of Lea and Perrins and gave them a recipe for a chutney that he had brought back from India. The firm duly made up a batch. But the Raj-retiree never returned and the chutney remained in the firm's store-room. Then, one day, the barrel containing the chutney exploded. The owners tasted the (now fermented) chutney, loved it and decided to sell it as a sauce. No mention was made of its Indian origins.

Or take the Nargisi Kofta. When visiting Brits try it at one of our restaurants, they say, "But it is like a Scotch Egg".

Ha!

The truth is that the Raj took Nargisi Kofta to the UK. The original dish had a gravy and that is how it was first served in Britain. Sir Walter Scott (of Ivanhoe fame) was an early fan and his enthusiasm for the dish led to it being called "Scotch Egg" because he was a Scot. Over time, the gravy vanished, the Brits forgot about the delicious mutton kebab filling and started using sausage meat instead and eventually, this great Indian dish became the industrial snack that you can pick up at every petrol station in the UK.

Mumbai has had better luck than most. The world has not stolen our dishes. In fact, they have added our city's name to dishes that we don't particularly regard as our own.

We are vaguely familiar with Bombay Halwa (though we may know it as Karachi Halwa) but I doubt if we would claim it as a great Mumbai dish. And what of Bombay Potatoes, an aloo sabzi so famous that even Jamie Oliver offers his own recipe? I have never heard the term used in our city.

And chivda? We like it but we recognise that every region of India has its own variation. In England however, it's seen as a Mumbai dish and even called Bombay Mix. (Like something created by a DJ!).

In fact, the only dish that has Bombay in its name and does actually come from here is Bombay Duck --- in all its variations. But even this is a joke. Because, as we know, Bombay Duck is not a bird at all but an Anglicisation of the bombil, a wonderful fish when eaten fresh. (I'm not so keen on the smelly, dried version).

The truth is that we, in Mumbai, are not so proud of individual dishes because, well, we have no ONE cuisine. Our skill as Bombaywallahs (Mumbaikars, Bombayites, Bambaiyas – take your pick!) is that we take things from around the world and we make them, just a little bit better.

Take bhelpuri. Chaat came to Mumbai from North India (UP probably) but we took the basic idea and created bhelpuri, India's greatest street food snack. Or take the hamburger or the sandwich. The vada pav is our reply to the hamburger. Our roadside sandwich is more delicious than anything you will find in a fancy restaurant.

One reason I love the Kala Ghoda Arts Festival is because it celebrates the genius of Mumbai. We are not a melting pot, we are a mosaic. We remain who we are and yet we fit into a larger whole.

Kala Ghoda, once --- and I hope again --- the centre of Mumbai remains the heart of the city. It is the Mumbai I grew up in, with its mix of Raj-era buildings, wonderful restaurants and the whiff of Arabian Sea air.

This book does not just have Mumbai recipes. You'll find everything here from a Spanish Paella to a Desi-Chinese crab cooked in a vaguely Mangalore style. This is only right. Mumbai has never been parochial. We like it all. And, as I never tire of saying, we make it just a little better.

Welcome to the mosaic. And happy cooking!

VIR SANGHVI

LEACH & WEBORNY

AUTHOR'S NOTE

Growing up amongst a family of food enthusiasts and fantastic cooks, one could not help but absorb a love for all things culinary. I may not be a professional chef but I do know my food and believe that it is one of the most interesting ways to break the ice and have a conversation. It's like Maya Angelou once said *"I'm just someone who likes cooking and for whom sharing food is a form of expression."*

I'm a foodie who can't stop experimenting with dishes I've tried. I have spent a considerable amount of my childhood (and adult life) eating my way through Kala Ghoda and the areas beyond. Its appeal lies not just in the restaurants, but in the architecture of the buildings, the quiet history that seeps out from under the metaphorical cobblestones and the pulse of art and culture within.

The Food vertical at the Kala Ghoda Arts Festival is a celebration of all things food and this book is an extension of that joy. Chefs from across the city have given us their best dishes, their signature dishes, simplified so that we can understand and cook them at home. I have been part of the Kala Ghoda Arts Festival since the inception of the Food vertical and each chef featured in this book is one whom I have wanted to learn from, one whom I look up to and whose food deserves a moment of gluttonous respect.

It has been five years of delicious goodness, heady smells and fresh, game changing food at the Kala Ghoda Arts Festival. There is no better time than this to bring you a book full of recipes from places in and around the Kala Ghoda area, as well as from chefs, restaurants and cafés that have been part of our festival. I hope you enjoy cooking with this book as much as I have enjoyed putting it together. Happy cooking!

NICOLE MODY

MENU

APPETIZERS

Achari Mushroom	38
Akuri	46
Beetroot Keftedes	98
Beetroot Microgreen Salad	62
Bok Choy Ramen Salad	86
Breakfast in a Bottle	44
Candied Pumpkin Soup	88
Classic Quiche Lorraine	20
Fried Bombay Duck	34
Gambas Al Ajillo	118
Goi Cuon	74
Hyderabadi Fish Tikka	32
Jaipuri Tikki	56
Japanese Prawn Tempura	76
Lobster Bisque	78
Mushroom Tea	116
Rock Shrimp Leche de Tigre	68
Som Tam Salad	72
Thai Fish Cakes	124

MAINS

Apple Wood-Smoked Chicken	92
Bangers and Mash	28
Beetroot Risotto	70
Brown Rice Paella	100
Butter Garlic Crab	36
Chicken Makhani	40
Corn Crêpe Raviolo	80
Gatte ka Pulao	58
Haleem	110
Khowsuey	94
Mewadi Kofta	60
Mushroom Gnocchi	90
Organic Wholegrain Pasta with Pesto	64
Pomegranate Molasses Salmon	120
Portuguese Roast Chicken	122
Spaghetti with Garden Vegetables	102
Tandoori Raan	42
Tamota Par Eeda	66

DESSERT

SANDWICHES

CONTENTS

ALL THINGS NICE, WITH A LOT OF SPICE!

Welcome to super culinary adventures at the Hindustan Times Kala Ghoda Arts Festival!

A WALK DOWN CULINARY LANE

It's easy for an enthusiastic foodie to spend a few days wandering through the streets around Kala Ghoda – there are so many different restaurants, cafés and stalls around! From a sugar cane juice stall across the Mumbai High Court to a tiny Goan kitchen in the bylanes of Colaba, one has to but step out of one's door to encounter a gastronomic smorgasbord.

1. Let's begin opposite the dilapidated Watson's Hotel building before moving down Rampart Row. The hustle and bustle of the working world emerges through Chetana's doors as diners tuck into the day's special *thali* – Gujarati, Maharashtrian or Rajasthani. Inhale the aroma of freshly baked bread at Serafina and pop in for a slice of their signature Margherita pizza. Stop and try the *reshmi chelo kebab* and *dal makhani* at Copper Chimney, or maybe the *chole bhature* from Bombay Blue.

Turn into the bylanes of Kala Ghoda and perk up with Kala Ghoda Café's homegrown teas, or their speciality chef's salad. Mamagoto's chicken and basil cups are a yummy snack to take you through the afternoon, as is Trishna's *prawn koliwada*. Dessert can be macarons at La Folie, the banana tart at The Pantry or a seven layer cookie at The Nutcracker. A chicken roll at Ayub's is a must for late night snackers.

2. We start our Irani café experience at Olympia Coffee House on Colaba Causeway for *kheema pao* and coffee. Get there early, they run out of the good stuff by 10 am! Walk past Regal Cinema and Lion Gate next to Horniman Circle to have *sali par eedu* and *jardaloo ma margi* at Jimmy Boy.

Spend some time admiring the beautiful architecture around you and wind your way along Ballard Estate to Britannia & Co. where you can enjoy a lemon soda, eat the *bombil fry* and berry pulao while chatting with your very friendly host. You then walk back towards Horniman Circle, past the iconic bright-red Bombay Samachar building to Yazdani Bakery for *bun-maska-chai*. Stroll into the bylanes of Flora Fountain by the Central Bank building and pick up *kheema sali* at Café Military or the prawn curry rice at Ideal Corner for dinner. Your Irani café experience culminates at Kyani & Co. with some Irani *chai*, *mawa* cake and *khari* biscuits.

3. Another exciting walk takes us through Colaba Causeway at lunchtime. We start with prawn pulao at New Martin Hotel next to Strand Cinema. We then walk onto the main road and pick up a chip butty from Theobroma, a shawarma from Sufra and a slice of Café Churchill's Bailey's cheesecake. Past the police station are our stops at Leopold Café for beef chilli fry and egg fried rice and at Delhi Darbar for the white chicken.

We sip a cold mug of beer at Café Mondegar and walk towards the Gateway of India to take in the colours of the sunset. Snack time starts at 7 pm at Bademiya with a *baida roti*, and at Bagdadi for the chicken fry with gravy. Dinner is at Ling's Pavilion for their famous Singapore chilli crab, finished off with honey noodles. Now, you're really done!

A HISTORY OF KALA GHODA

Mumbai city has always had unexpected whimsy when naming its neighbourhoods. The junction from Walkeshwar to Malabar Hill is known as Teen Batti, named for the three-armed lamp that lights the sloping turn. Part of the Fort area is referred to as 'Fountain' because the Flora Fountain stands in the middle of the area. We have oddly specific names for oddly specific places like the AC Market and Null Bazaar but maybe the most recognizable of these Mumbai neighbourhoods is the iconic Kala Ghoda.

A black equestrian statue of King Edward VII, then the Prince of Wales, once stood where the central parking lot in front of Rhythm House is today. The square and its surrounding crescent-shaped zone were affectionately dubbed Kala Ghoda. The city's iconography was vastly and emotionally altered when the statue was removed in 1965 in a drive to rid the then city of Bombay of its Colonial relics and the Kala Ghoda was relocated to the Byculla zoo. It has been said that MF Hussain was so distraught that the statue was being moved that he borrowed paper and mapping ink from the Pundole Art Gallery nearby to paint the Kala Ghoda, an icon that became so influential and significant to his style that it popped up on his canvases throughout his career.

Half a century has passed since this statue has been moved but its presence looms greater than ever. Not only has the name stuck, it has become synonymous with a neighbourhood that is now best known as the heartland of art, culture and, of course, food in Mumbai, even for generations that have never seen the actual statue.

Kala Ghoda's affair with the arts can be traced back to the late sixties when Mumbai's young and hungry poets, led by Arun Kolatkar, would congregate at the Wayside Inn on Rampart Row to write, discuss and drink. Dr. Ambedkar once worked on the Constitution of India whilst sitting at the very same Wayside Inn. Until recently, the Jehangir Art Gallery housed Usha Khanna's homespun Samovar where artists and poets would regularly hang out. Hussain, Gaitonde, Ara, Sabavala, Ezekiel, Jussawala and the much-loved Behram "Busybee" Contractor haunted the tables of the popular café.

Today, in 2016, the Wayside Inn and Samovar are no more but like the Kala Ghoda they have left a legacy of young, rebellious artists who have adopted the area as their hub of expression. With the new guard of burgeoning independent art galleries, artisanal stores, restaurants and cafés integrating seamlessly with the old landmarks one would be hard-pressed to find a neighbourhood in the world where Neo-Gothic, Neo-Classical, Indo-Saracenic and plain old modern hipster play so well together. Kala Ghoda has become the epicentre of free expression through art in Modern India.

The Kala Ghoda Association, a collection of artists, historians, patrons, philanthropists and preservationists was formed on the 30th of October, 1998. Its mission was simple: maintain, preserve and enhance the heritage and art of South Mumbai through the Kala Ghoda conduit.

Through these guardians of the artsy galaxy came the Kala Ghoda Arts Festival, which has grown over the years to embrace the best of the country's creative zeitgeist. Galleries play host to exhibits, talks, debates and readings while Rampart Row is transformed into a visual delight of art installations and a shopper's paradise with independent artists selling their wares. Film screenings, plays and concerts pepper the area and the food of Kala Ghoda takes the revelry to another level. From classics like a Chetana *thali* to the nouveau sugar star La Folié, there's something for everyone.

Come February, for 9 days this cultural milestone of Mumbai throbs with pageantry amidst a backdrop of antiquity.

Ye hedonists arise.

FOOD AT THE KALA GHODA ARTS FESTIVAL

A new offering was cooked up and served during the 2012 Kala Ghoda Arts Festival: Food. Designed to bring the art of cooking to domestic kitchens, the first year of this section saw eight of Mumbai's most acknowledged chefs demonstrate their wizardry and culinary talent.

Within days, word spread like pâté and the multitude that attended each workshop poured like honey over the block.

While the festival is essentially a come one, come all pageant, the indoor space constraints for these demonstrations compel certain exclusivity. There have been times when hopeful attendees jostle others into outer space!

Prominent eateries from across the city put their best cook forward. The restaurateur, blogger, entrepreneur, home cook – each has become part of the Kala Ghoda household. The audience is family now and we have seen many of the same faces in the crowd each year; sometimes even the same crowd of different faces. Discerning culinary enthusiasts all, they have helped shape the food vertical for what it is.

Over the years the city's best chefs have demonstrated their finest recipes, simplified for a home audience: Rahul Akerkar, Alex Sanchez, Moshe Shek, Milind Sovani, Nikhil Chib, Pooja Dhingra, Vicky Ratnani, Irfan Pabaney, Viraf Patel, Rachel Goenka Khetarpal, Aashiyana Shroff, Thomas Zacharias, Gresham Fernandes, Mukhtar Qureshi, Asha Khatau, Vikas Seth and Zeba Kohli. Who's next?

IN AND AROUND

THE TABLE
Chetana
CHETANA
RAMPART ROW
BUSABA
Trishna
TRISHNA
KALA GHODA CAFE

KALA GHODA

CLASSIC QUICHE LORRAINE

A traditional savoury tart from the North-Eastern regions of France, whose buttery, flaky crust goes perfectly with a rich, creamy filling and earthy Gruyere cheese.

SERVES 1

FOR THE FILLING

40 ml milk
40 ml cream
20 grams ham, diced
20 grams Gruyere or any sharp cheese, shredded
1 egg
1 teaspoon unsalted butter
Salt and pepper to taste

FOR THE DOUGH

25 grams organic flour
12.5 grams soft butter
1 teaspoon water

Preheat your oven to 200°C

Butter and flour a 4-inch tart mould with a removable bottom.

1. To make the dough, rub the butter and organic flour together between your fingers until it resembles coarse breadcrumbs.
2. Add water a few drops at a time, and knead the flour until it becomes an even and flexible little ball of dough. Cling wrap and refrigerate for an hour.
3. Turn the dough out onto a well-floured surface and roll out to an even thickness of 5 mm.
4. Lay the dough out carefully over the tart mould, pressing down from the centre outwards. Make sure there are no air bubbles trapped between the dough and the mould. Prick the bottom with a fork and refrigerate until you need it.
5. To make the filling, mix the milk, cream and egg together and whisk quickly with a fork. Add a pinch of salt and pepper and mix well.
6. Remove the quiche base from the fridge and drizzle the shredded Gruyere and diced ham over the base. Pour the well-mixed milk filling into the tart.
7. Bake the quiche for 20 to 30 minutes, until it has turned golden brown.
8. Serve warm with a garden-fresh salad.

BHAVNAGARI CHILLI PESTO CHICKEN SANDWICH

Bhavnagari chillis are usually stuffed, fried and served as *bhajias*. An interesting spicy twist on pesto, combined with spicy focaccia and grilled chicken brings this underappreciated chilli to life.

SERVES 1

30 grams butter
2 teaspoons black pepper, crushed
1 piece chicken breast, boneless
1 piece spicy focaccia bread
1 onion, sliced thinly
2 tablespoons tomato relish (page 132)
A handful of rocket lettuce
Salt to taste

FOR THE PESTO

100 grams Bhavnagari chilli
20 grams cashew nuts
30 ml olive oil
1 teaspoon green peppercorns
2 cloves garlic, peeled
½ teaspoon salt

---

1. To make the Bhavnagari chilli pesto, place the cashew nuts, Bhavnagari chilli, salt and green peppercorns together in a mixer and blend.
2. Clean the chicken breast and marinate it with salt and pepper and a teaspoon of the Bhavnagari pesto. Grill evenly on both sides.
3. Slice the focaccia into two pieces and butter them both.
4. Layer the bread with rocket lettuce and the sliced onion. Spoon more Bhavnagari pesto over the grilled chicken and place it on the focaccia.
5. Close the sandwich and toast lightly before serving.
6. Serve with homemade tomato relish, mustard and a side salad.

FLOURLESS CHOCOLATE CAKE

This richly decadent cake develops a delicately crisp crust while allowing the warm chocolate centre to remain moist and fudgy. Comfort food at its best.

SERVES 8

195 grams 70% dark chocolate, rough chopped
180 grams unsalted butter
180 grams castor sugar
5 large eggs

Preheat your oven to 180°C

Butter and flour a 9-inch springform cake tin with a removable base.

1. Melt the 70% dark chocolate and unsalted butter together in a small saucepan over a low flame making sure they have mixed well.
2. Beat the eggs and castor sugar together until they are pale and fluffy and the mixture has thickened.
3. Gently fold in the cooled chocolate mixture and incorporate thoroughly.
4. Pour the batter into your prepared cake tin and bake for 25 minutes. Unlike most cakes, this one will not rise as much as it will thicken and richen.
5. You will know the cake is done when a skewer inserted into the middle comes out clean.
6. Serve warm with a dusting of icing sugar and a few curls of orange zest.

DOUBLE CHEDDAR BURGER

A combination of three cuts of meat brings the double Cheddar burger to the forefront of must-eat and must-make burgers in Mumbai.

SERVES 1

FOR THE PATTY

- 80 grams water buffalo undercut
- 45 grams water buffalo rib eye
- 35 grams water buffalo brisket
- 20 grams softened butter
- 1 teaspoon black pepper, crushed
- 1 tablespoon fresh thyme
- 10 ml oil
- 1 burger bun
- 1 tomato, sliced into rounds
- ¼ onion, sliced into rounds
- 1 thick slice mature Cheddar
- 2 tablespoons garlic butter
- 1 teaspoon salt
- 1 portion French fries
- A handful of romaine lettuce, shredded

---

1. Mix the ground undercut, rib eye and brisket with the softened butter, black pepper, thyme and oil in a bowl until just combined. Be careful not to knead or massage the meat too intensely or you will spoil the texture. Add a pinch of salt.
2. Form the meat into a circular patty by placing it in your hand and shaping it. Cling wrap the patty and chill it for 20 to 30 minutes to allow the meat to combine.
3. Grill or pan-fry each side of the burger patty for 2 to 3 minutes until it is browned and cooked. If you prefer a more well done patty, you may continue cooking it for another 5 to 6 minutes.
4. Cut your burger bun in two and smear garlic butter on both sides. Toast on a pan until the bun is crispy.
5. Layer the bottom half of the bun with lettuce and place your grilled patty on top.
6. Add the onion and sliced tomato.
7. Place a thick slice of Cheddar on the other half of the bun and put it back on the pan to melt slightly. Close the bun with a long wooden holder.
8. Serve with French fries and a chilled drink.
9. For maximum enjoyment, eat this with your hands.

BANGERS AND MASH

Spicy garlic sausages are placed on a bed of creamy mustard mash, topped with caramelised onions and a light red wine rosemary sauce. This is pub grub at its simplest and most delicious.

SERVES 1

2 large garlic krakauer sausages
60 grams caramelised onion
1 tablespoon butter
1 tablespoon oil
A handful of fresh rosemary
¼ cup red wine rosemary sauce (page 132)

FOR THE MASH

200 grams potato, boiled
15 ml cream
2 tablespoons softened butter
2 tablespoons mustard
1 teaspoon salt
A handful of fresh parsley

1. Peel and mash the boiled potato with a potato masher while hot and squish through a sieve to avoid lumps.
2. Melt butter in a pan and add the cream and salt. Fold in the mashed potatoes and whisk until smooth. If you're happy with regular mash, stop at this stage and season with chopped parsley.
3. You can alternatively add 2 tablespoons mustard to the mash along with some salt and pepper. Voila! Mustard Mash.
4. Grill your sausages on a hot griddle as per the instructions given on the package.
5. To assemble, layer the mashed potato on a flat plate and place the grilled sausages on top.
6. Sprinkle the caramelised onion and spoon the red wine jus sauce around.
7. Strew a handful of rosemary over the top and serve.

BHUT JOLOKIA BURGER

A tribute to the world's second hottest chilli, this fiery-red grilled chicken patty is coated with bhut jolokia sauce, topped with jalapeños and lettuce and is not for the faint of heart.

SERVES 1

FOR THE PATTY

- 150 grams boneless chicken breast
- 1 tablespoon salt
- 1 tablespoon black pepper, crushed
- 1 tablespoon smoked paprika
- 1 tablespoon vegetable oil
- 1 tablespoon bhut jolokia sauce
- 1 tablespoon tomato ketchup
- ¼ cup refined flour
- A handful of basil
- 2 tablespoons garlic butter
- 2 tablespoons bhut jolokia mayonnaise (page 132)
- 1 multigrain burger bun
- ¼ cup mustard
- A handful of fresh lollo rosso lettuce
- Sweet potato fries
- Fresh coleslaw

---

1. Pat the chicken down with kitchen paper to make sure it is dry.
2. Mix the salt, pepper, oil, paprika and basil together in a bowl and spread it evenly over the chicken.
3. Combine the bhut jolokia sauce with tomato ketchup and spread thinly over the marinated chicken. Allow this to sit for 10 minutes.
4. Sift flour, salt and pepper together in a bowl and dust the chicken patty in it evenly.
5. Heat some oil in a heavy-bottomed pan.
6. Fry the chicken until it is golden brown.
7. Dip the fried chicken back into the ketchup and bhut jolokia mixture to achieve a higher level of spice
8. Cut your burger bun in two and smear garlic butter on both sides. Toast on a pan until the bun is crispy.
9. Layer the lollo rosso lettuce on the base and top it with your fried bhut jolokia chicken patty. Close the bun with a long wooden holder.
10. Serve with mustard, bhut jolokia mayonnaise, sweet potato fries and some cooling coleslaw.

HYDERABADI FISH TIKKA

Succulent fillets of pomfret are lovingly encrusted with crushed black pepper and cooked to tender steamy perfection. A twist on the usual tandoori masala that most prefer, these *tikkas* will quickly become a party favourite.

SERVES 2

6 pomfret fillets, with skin

FOR THE MARINADE

½ teaspoon salt
¼ teaspoon turmeric powder
2 tablespoons black pepper, crushed
1 tablespoon lime juice
Salt to taste

---

1. Clean the pomfret fillets thoroughly making sure that the skin is intact on one side. You can use either pomfret or *rawas* for this recipe.
2. Mix the salt, turmeric powder and lime juice together in a small bowl and marinate the cleaned fillets.
3. Encrust each fillet individually with the crushed pepper.
4. Cook the fish in a home tandoor on medium heat until a toothpick inserted in the fish comes out clean.
5. Serve the *tikkas* with flaky butter *naan* and a squeeze of lime.

FRIED BOMBAY DUCK

A local Mumbai favourite, this fish is moist and flaky on the inside and contrasts sharply with its crispy golden crust. You can find Bombay duck, or *bombil* as it is referred to, on menus of most seafood restaurants.

SERVES 2

4	Bombay duck
1	cup rice flour
1-2	litres vegetable oil

FOR THE MARINADE

½	teaspoon ginger-garlic paste
¼	teaspoon turmeric powder
½	teaspoon red chilli powder
½	teaspoon salt

1. Clean and slit the *bombil* into two halves leaving the spine intact.
2. Wrap the fish in a clean kitchen cloth and weigh it down with a frying pan or a similarly heavy object. This allows the kitchen cloth to absorb the water from the fish, giving it a flaky texture.
3. Mix the ginger-garlic paste, turmeric powder, red chilli powder and salt together in a small bowl and set aside.
4. Once the fish has dried out completely, spread the marinade over it and let it stand for at least 3 hours.
5. Heat oil in a deep frying pan until it is smoking, making sure that you have enough oil in the pan to cover the fish completely.
6. Coat the *bombil* evenly with rice flour and fry each piece of fish until golden brown. Place on a paper towel to absorb excess oil.
7. Serve the *bombil* immediately with sliced onion and wedges of lime.

04
ILL ON HIM
TECH-IT
IT eats
students
SOLUT

BUTTER GARLIC CRAB

Though a Mangalorean dish, a trip to Mumbai is not complete without eating the butter garlic crab at one of the city's more popular seafood restaurants. Butter garlic crab is commonly eaten with *neer* dosa, a light crêpe prepared from rice batter, and one's hands. Don't be afraid to get messy!

SERVES 2

1	medium sized crab, cleaned
100	grams butter
5-10	cloves garlic, finely chopped
	Salt and white pepper to taste

1. To make the butter garlic sauce, melt the butter in a *kadhai* on low heat.
2. Add your pieces of finely chopped garlic just before the butter starts to froth. Be careful not to allow the butter to brown or the sauce will need to be redone.
3. Add salt and white pepper to the sauce and adjust the seasoning as needed.
4. To steam the crab, place a large half-filled pot of water to boil. Put a circular rack inside the pot of water to hold the crab as it steams. You can also use a home steamer if you have one.
5. Once the water has come to a boil, place the crab on the rack and cover the pot. Allow the crab to steam for 15 to 20 minutes until the shell turns orange.
6. Using a pair of tongs, add the steamed crab to the *kadhai* of delicious butter garlic sauce and toss it around until the crab is completely covered.
7. Serve hot with soft *neer* dosa and dig in.

ACHARI MUSHROOM

Made with spices that are typically used for pickling in North India, this recipe is flavourful and delicious. It is simple enough to cook at a moment's notice (if you have the ingredients on hand of course!) and tastes as good at home as it does in a restaurant.

SERVES 4

200	grams fresh mushrooms
2	red bell peppers
2	yellow bell peppers
2	tablespoons *achar* paste
¼	teaspoon *ajwain*
2	tablespoons gram flour
2	tablespoons oil
¼	teaspoon green chilli, chopped
¼	teaspoon ginger, chopped
¼	teaspoon garlic, chopped
½	teaspoon coriander, chopped

1. Wash the mushrooms in running water and dry them on kitchen paper. Cut the red and yellow bell peppers into 2-inch cubes.
2. Heat some oil in a frying pan and add the green chilli, ginger, garlic, coriander and gram flour to it. Cook this for 2 minutes allowing the ingredients to mix properly.
3. Combine the gram flour mixture with the *achar* paste and *ajwain* in a large bowl.
4. Marinate your mushrooms and cut peppers in the mixture for around 10 minutes.
5 Arrange the mushrooms and bell peppers on skewers, starting with the bell peppers. To get a nice riot of colour, slot one red bell pepper, one yellow bell pepper and a mushroom on the skewer and repeat.
6. Cook the skewers on a preheated barbecue or home tandoor for 7 to 8 minutes. You can also cook these at home on a griddle pan, simply add a small piece of heated charcoal to the pan and cover to get a smoky texture on the vegetables.
7. Serve with mint chutney and a squeeze of lime.

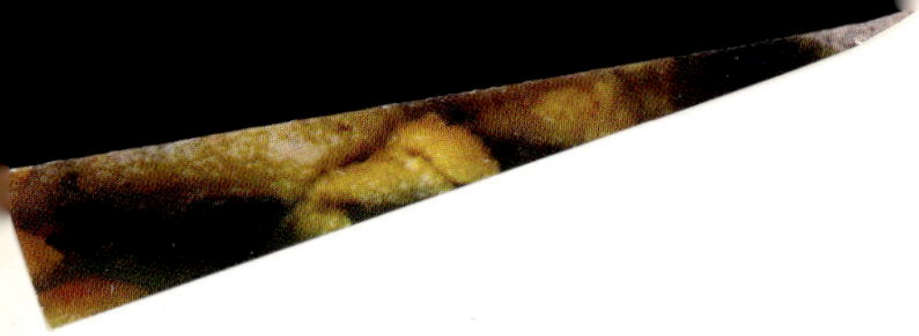

CHICKEN MAKHANI

No dish has gained the popularity and notoriety that chicken makhani, also known as butter chicken or chicken makhanwala has in India. Created in the 1950s, there are several accounts of people coming to blows over disagreements about whose recipe was better, and several other stories of people trying to STEAL one another's secret recipes.

SERVES 4

1 whole tandoori chicken
1 cup tomato purée
4 onions, chopped
2 tablespoons ginger-garlic paste
1 teaspoon turmeric powder
½ teaspoon *shahi jeera*
1 teaspoon coriander powder
1 teaspoon cumin powder
1 teaspoon *garam* masala powder
2 tablespoons oil
2 tablespoons cashew nut paste
2 tablespoons Kashmiri chilli paste
¼ cup cream
¼ teaspoon *kasturi methi*
4 tablespoons butter
¼ cup water
Salt to taste

1. Debone the chicken and shred it into long pieces.
2. Heat the oil in a wide deep-bottom pan and add the *shahi jeera*. Stir until it starts crackling and add the chopped onions, frying them until they are golden brown.
3. Add the ginger-garlic paste, coriander powder, cumin powder, *garam* masala powder and turmeric powder to the onions. Mix well and continue to cook for a few minutes.
4. Add the tomato purée and cook for another 5 minutes.
5. Once the masala has mixed, add the Kashmiri chilli and cashew nut paste and cook until it starts secreting oil.
6. Add your chicken pieces and ¼ cup of water. Allow it to simmer until the gravy becomes thick.
7. Top with butter, cream and *kasturi methi* just before serving.
8. Serve hot with *naan* or rice.

TANDOORI RAAN

This dish takes some practice to get right. A tender leg of lamb is marinated overnight with spices and curd and roasted until the meat is falling of the bone.

SERVES 6

1 lamb leg, approximately 1 kilo in weight
5 tablespoons papaya paste
2 tablespoons ginger-garlic paste

FOR THE MARINADE

1 cup onions, fried
2 onions, chopped
4 tablespoons *khus khus* paste
1 tablespoon almond paste
2 tablespoons cashew nut paste
3 tablespoons Kashmiri chilli paste
2 tablespoons *garam* masala powder
4 tablespoons salad oil
1 cup curd
Salt to taste

---

1. Clean and make deep slits on the leg of lamb. Marinate it with the ginger-garlic and papaya paste and place it aside for at least 4 hours.
2. Blend your ingredients for the masala together in a grinder – the onions, *khus khus* paste, almond paste, cashew nut paste, Kashmiri chilli paste, *garam* masala powder, salad oil, curd and a pinch of salt.
3. Rub the marinade all over the lamb and allow it to continue marinating for a few hours or overnight.
4. When you are ready to begin cooking, preheat your oven to 200oC.
5. Place the lamb leg in a heavy baking pan and cover it with a lid or aluminium foil. Roast it for 45 minutes, turning it from time to time.
6. Remove the lid or foil covering for the last 10 minutes to allow the masala to brown.
7. When the mutton is tender and almost falling off the bone, serve it hot with rotis, thinly sliced onion rings, mint chutney and wedges of lime.

BREAKFAST IN A BOTTLE

Breakfast in a bottle is a wholesome, delicious and easy way to kick-start your day. A fully loaded breakfast on the go made with milk, oats, granola, honey and fruit, will keep your energy levels high all morning.

SERVES 1

120 ml milk
4 dates
2 tablespoons oats
1 tablespoon mixed nuts
1 teaspoon honey
1 tablespoon granola
Mangoes, strawberries, raspberries

---

1. Heat the milk in a saucepan and lightly cook the oats. You are looking for a watery consistency that is *not* traditional porridge.

   OR

   Soak the oats and dates in hot milk and refrigerate overnight once cooled.

2. Add the dates and let them soak in the warm milk and oats mixture until they soften.
3. Once cooled down, add this mixture, along with granola, honey and nuts to a blender with 2 cubes of ice. Blend until you have a smooth almost silky consistency.
4. Adding fruit to this recipe gives it a deliciously zingy kick. Try fruit like mango or strawberries when in season.

AKURI

The Parsi version of *bhurji* brings together eggs, onion, tomato and a host of spices that are reminiscent of waking up to the whiff of egg and hot *brun pao* on a Lonavala weekend away.

SERVES 2

2	large eggs
½	tomato, finely chopped
1	small green chilli, finely chopped
1	small onion, finely chopped
1	teaspoon ginger-garlic paste
1	teaspoon coriander, chopped
1	teaspoon butter
½	teaspoon turmeric powder
½	teaspoon red paprika powder
	Salt to taste

1. Finely chop your tomato, onions, coriander and green chillies.
2. Heat some oil in a non-stick pan and cook the ginger garlic-paste until brown. Add the onions and cook until they are translucent.
3. Add the tomato, green chilli, red paprika and turmeric powder and continue cooking for 5 minutes. You want to make sure that you cook the spices through to avoid a very strong taste in your eggs.
4. In a mixing bowl, lightly beat the eggs with coriander and add them to the pan. Turn the heat down and keep stirring.
5. Cook your *akuri* till a creamy consistency is achieved, stirring continuously. Do not overcook the eggs to a scramble.
6. Season with salt to taste and top with a squeeze of lime and chopped coriander.

CHUNKY MUSHROOM BURGER

This chunky mushroom burger with Harissa mayonnaise is a refreshing option for veggies who are tired of eating potato patties. The combination of mushroom and cheese brings an earthiness to this burger that is missing in other vegetarian burgers.

SERVES 1

FOR THE PATTY

50 grams Portobello mushrooms, rough chopped
25 grams red Cheddar, grated
25 grams Mozzarella, grated
20 grams olives
1 teaspoon chilli flakes
1 teaspoon parsley
2 tablespoons breadcrumbs
2 tablespoons all-purpose flour
1 burger bun
1-2 litres vegetable oil
1 tomato, sliced into rounds
1/4 onion, sliced into rounds
2 tablespoons Harissa mayonnaise (page 132)
A handful of fresh lettuce

1. Place the mushrooms, Cheddar, Mozzarella, olives, parsley, chilli flakes and salt in a big bowl and mix well. Use your hands and make sure that the ingredients really blend together.
2. Add a handful of breadcrumbs to the mix and begin to form the patty. It should form into a rough disc the size of your palm and 3 cm thick. Use the extra breadcrumbs to bind the outside.
3. Wrap the patty lightly with cling wrap and refrigerate for at least 2 hours.
4. Mix the flour with a few tablespoons of water or soda to make a thin paste. Dip the patty into this batter and then cover it with breadcrumbs once again.
5. Deep fry or pan fry the patty until the outside is crisp and golden. Place it on a paper towel to remove the excess oil.
6. To assemble, slice the burger bun in half and butter it lightly. Warm slightly and spread a thin layer of the Harissa mayonnaise on each half.
7. Layer the bottom with lettuce and place the patty on top.
8. Spread a spoon of Harissa mayonnaise on top and add a few slices of onion and tomato.
9. Cover with bun lid and serve with fries or potato chips. Prepare to be wowed.

DAMASK

A delicate rose Bavarian mousse with raspberry and lychee compote and a light Chantilly, this dessert's flavours are subtle and distinct, and very light on the palate.

SERVES 4

FOR THE CHANTILLY ROSE CREAM

200 grams whipped cream
200 grams mascarpone cream
20 grams icing sugar
1-2 teaspoons natural rose essence
20 grams rose syrup
2 cups fresh raspberries
1 cup fresh lychees
1 ready vanilla sponge cake
White chocolate shards
A handful of fresh rose petals

1. Whip your cream and icing sugar with the mascarpone, adding the natural rose essence and rose syrup once the sugar is blended.
2. Chill the cream and rose mixture in the fridge for 20 minutes so that it is stable enough to layer on the vanilla cake.
3. Using a sharp knife or kitchen thread, cut the vanilla sponge cake into 3 thin discs.
4. Gently spread each layer with the crème Chantilly and sprinkle a handful of raspberries and lychees over it.
5. Carefully stack each layer one on top of the other.
6. Ice the cake completely with the remaining crème Chantilly.
7. Garnish the damask with chocolate shards on the sides and top with fresh rose petals.
8. If you enjoy a moist cake and a strong rose flavour, brush the sponges generously with rose syrup before adding the crème Chantilly.

GRANDMA'S CARROT PATCH

Soft carrot cake sits atop a biscuit crumb accompanied by warm apricot marmalade, carrot cream cheese mousse and fresh lemon cream. This is carrot cake like you've never eaten before!

SERVES 4

FOR THE BISCUIT BASE

50 grams butter
150 grams digestive biscuit, crushed

FOR THE CARROT CAKE

200 grams sugar
150 grams vegetable oil
2 large eggs
130 grams flour
1 teaspoon baking powder
1½ teaspoons cinnamon powder
4 medium carrots, finely grated
60 grams walnuts, crushed

FOR THE CARROT CREAM CHEESE MOUSSE

5 tablespoons sugar
25 ml water
2 egg yolks
3 teaspoons icing sugar
1 packet Philadelphia cream cheese
3 medium carrots, puréed
5 grams gelatin
1¼ cups whipped cream

FOR THE LEMON CREAM

80 ml freshly squeezed lemon juice
62 grams butter
3 eggs
125 ml whipped cream
Zest of 2 lemons

---

1. To make the biscuit base, mix your ingredients together in a food processor until the mixture resembles wet sand. Press evenly onto a baking sheet and bake at 170°C for 10 to 12 minutes. Cut the biscuit into rectangular pieces 3 cm x 11 cm in diameter and keep aside.
2. Meanwhile to make the carrot cake, beat the eggs and sugar until pale and fluffy. Sift together the flour, baking powder and cinnamon powder and fold into the eggs. Pour in the oil and add the grated carrot and walnuts. Mix thoroughly.
3. Line a baking sheet and spread the batter thinly. Bake at 180°C for 10 to 15 minutes. Once it has cooled, cut it into three layers 3 cm x 11 cm in diameter.
4. For the mousse, whisk the egg yolks, water and sugar together in a glass bowl set over a pot of boiling water. Whisk until the mixture is satiny yellow and forms thick ribbons when lifted with a spoon. Allow it to cool down in an ice bath. Melt the cream cheese, icing sugar, gelatin and carrot purée and fold it into the cooled sabayon. Gently fold in the whipped cream.
5. Combine the butter, cream, lemon juice, eggs and lemon zest in a saucepan and whisk constantly over medium heat until the mixture thickens and coats the back of a spoon thickly (do not boil). Strain into a bowl once cool.
6. To assemble, layer each piece of the carrot cake with apricot jam, carrot mousse and lemon cream. Place one on top of the other and freeze. Place the cake on the biscuit base and serve with a flourish.

MANGO VELOUR

Under a vibrant yellow dome is a layer of airy Genoise cake, topped with fresh mango, finished with luxurious mango Philadelphia créme Chantilly.

SERVES 4

600 grams whipping cream
50 grams castor sugar
100 grams mango pulp
2 grams agar agar
1 packet Philadelphia cream cheese
Freshly chopped mangoes

FOR THE VANILLA CAKE BASE

37 grams all-purpose flour
1 teaspoon baking powder
125 ml water
125 ml vegetable oil
185 grams castor sugar
60 grams buttermilk
1 tablespoon apple cider vinegar
½ teaspoon baking soda
1 teaspoon vanilla extract
A pinch of salt

Preheat your oven to 180°C

Prepare and line 4 cupcake moulds.

1. Boil the whipping cream in a small pan and dissolve the agar agar. Add the castor sugar and mango pulp and mix well.
2. Let the mixture set in the refrigerator for 1½ hours.
3. Once cold, beat the mixture with cream cheese until smooth and fluffy enough to pipe in a piping bag.
4. To make the vanilla cake base, cream the butter and castor sugar in a bowl.
5. Add the buttermilk and water and mix together very slowly with a whisk.
6. Sift the flour, baking powder and salt together and fold into the batter carefully, without losing too much volume.
7. Dissolve the baking soda in apple cider vinegar and add to the batter along with the vanilla extract.
8. Pour the batter into the cupcake moulds, going no higher than ⅔ of the way up.
9. Bake for 20 minutes and then allow the cakes to cool.
10. Once the bases are cooled slice the crust off the cakes. These form the base of your mango velour.
11. Slice fresh mangoes and place them on each base.
12. Pipe the créme Chantilly on top of the mangoes with a rose nozzle tip.

JAIPURI TIKKI

A combination of staples found in every Indian kitchen, these *tikkis* are the perfect snack to serve with masala *chai* on a rainy day.

SERVES 4

6	medium-sized potatoes, boiled
2	carrots, chopped
50	grams green peas
50	grams paneer
50	grams rice flour
¾	cup vegetable oil
½	teaspoon cumin seeds
1	teaspoon green chilli paste
½	teaspoon turmeric powder
½	teaspoon coriander powder
½	teaspoon black pepper
½	teaspoon sugar
	Salt to taste

1. Peel and mash the boiled potatoes until they are smooth. Boil the carrots and green peas.
2. Blend the paneer, green peas and carrot pieces together until you have a smooth paste.
3. Heat some oil in a heavy-bottomed pan. Add the cumin seeds and wait for them to 'pop'. Once they pop, lower the heat and add the green chilli paste, turmeric powder, coriander and black pepper. Stir for a few seconds and quickly add the carrot, pea and paneer paste.
4. Mix well, making sure the spices have been folded into the paste. Add sugar and salt to taste and put aside.
5. To form the *tikkis*, take a spoonful of mashed potato and place it in the palm of your hand. Pat it into a circular cup and put one teaspoon of the paneer mixture into it. Close the cup from all sides to form a *tikki* and place on a wet cloth.
6. Continue doing this until you have used all your mixture. You should have approximately 10 *tikkis*.
7. Heat a little oil in a non-stick pan. Pat the *tikkis* with rice flour and fry one at a time. Shallow fry them until they are golden brown on both sides and serve hot with masala *chai*.

Best for a rainy day!

GATTE KA PULAO

A rustic Indian *pulao* with gram flour dumplings, inspired by the deserts of Rajasthan, is served on festive occasions in place of steamed rice.

SERVES 4

FOR THE GATTAS

150 grams Bengal gram flour
1 teaspoon aniseed
1 teaspoon omum seed
2 teaspoons curd
1 teaspoon chilli powder
50 ml vegetable oil
Salt to taste

FOR THE PULAO

250 grams basmati rice
25 ml vegetable oil
2 medium-sized onions, chopped
3 cloves
2 cardamom pods
1 teaspoon cumin seeds
½ teaspoon mustard seeds
½ teaspoon turmeric powder
½ teaspoon chilli powder
1 pinch of asafoetida
A handful of coriander leaves, chopped
Salt to taste

Pre soak the rice in water for 2 hours.

1. Mix the flour, aniseed, omum seeds, curd, chilli powder, oil and salt together in a bowl.
2. Add a few tablespoons of water and knead to a stiff dough. Divide the dough into six equal portions and shape each into a 12 cm long cylindrical roll.
3. Bring a pot of water to boil and put in all 6 rolls of dough. Cook them for 10 minutes.
4. Once the dough has cooled down, cut into smaller pieces that are approximately 1 cm in height.
5. Heat vegetable oil in a pan and deep-fry the *gattas* until golden. Place them on a paper towel to drain.
6. Heat some oil in a deep pot. Add the cloves, cardamom, cumin seeds, mustard seeds and asafoetida and sauté for 1 minute. Add chopped onion and continue to sauté until golden brown.
7. Add the turmeric and chilli powders, cooked *gatta* and the pre-soaked rice. Stir well.
8. Add enough water to cover the rice and cook until it is done. Make sure that there is enough water or the rice grains will be lumpy.
9. Garnish the *pulao* with chopped coriander leaves and serve hot.

MEWADI KOFTA

Vegetable stuffed dumplings are served on a bed of richly spiced gravy and will fill you with warmth on a cold winter's day.

SERVES 4

FOR THE KOFTAS

50	grams green beans, boiled
50	grams green peas, boiled
2	small potatoes, boiled and peeled
100	grams paneer, grated
1	carrot, boiled
1	teaspoon *garam* masala powder
½	teaspoon turmeric powder
1	teaspoon coriander powder
1	teaspoon chilli powder
½	teaspoon cumin powder
25	grams cornflour
200	ml oil

FOR THE GRAVY

2	medium-sized onions, finely chopped
½	teaspoon cumin seeds
½	teaspoon turmeric powder
1	teaspoon chilli powder
1	teaspoon *garam* masala powder
3	tomatoes, skinned and puréed
50	grams cashew nut paste
50	ml oil
	A handful of coriander leaves, chopped
	Salt to taste

1. Mash the vegetables, potatoes and grated paneer together, making sure the mash is not too smooth. Lumps help when making the *koftas*.
2. Heat some oil in a frying pan and fry the *garam* masala, turmeric, coriander, cumin and chilli powders. Add salt and stir for a few seconds to avoid burning.
3. Add the mashed mixture of potatoes, vegetables and paneer and mix thoroughly.
4 Add cornflour and stir well. Remove from the heat.
5. Divide the mixture and roll into lemon-sized *koftas* or dumplings.
6. Heat oil in a pan and deep-fry the *koftas* until golden. Drain and reserve.
7. For the gravy, heat some oil in a pan and fry your chopped onions till golden brown.
8. Add cumin seeds. When they 'pop', add turmeric, chilli and *garam* masala powders and stir quickly.
9. Add the tomato purée and cashew nut paste. Stir till the colour changes and add enough water to make the gravy. Simmer for a while and then add salt to taste.
10. Arrange the fried *koftas* in the gravy. Stir gently to avoid breaking them. Garnish with chopped coriander leaves.
11. Serve hot.

BEETROOT MICROGREEN SALAD

A garden-fresh salad is topped with a poached egg and vibrant microgreens. This delicious salad is a nutrient powerhouse that is perfect for a light lunch.

SERVES 2

1 large beetroot
1 cup mixed organic microgreens
¼ cup roasted walnuts, rough chopped
½ cup goat's cheese, roasted
A handful of fresh mixed lettuce leaves

FOR THE POACHED EGG

1 fresh egg
1 tablespoon vinegar
1 teaspoon rock salt

FOR THE DRESSING

1 cup extra virgin olive oil
3 tablespoons vinegar
1 tablespoon lime juice
Salt and pepper to taste

Preheat your oven to 180°C

1. Drizzle a little olive oil and sea salt over the beetroot and wrap it in some foil.
2. Place it on a baking tray and roast the beetroot for 45 minutes.
3. To make the salad dressing, combine the olive oil, vingegar and lime juice in a small bowl. Add the salt and pepper cautiously at the end, making sure not to overpower the flavour.
4. Add a tablespoon of vinegar to a pot of salted water and bring it up to a rolling boil.
5. With a spoon, swirl the water around to create a mini tornado in the centre of the pot and crack your egg into it. This helps keep the egg white together as it poaches. Allow it to cook for 3 to 4 minutes and remove with a slotted spoon.
6. To assemble, mix the lettuce leaves with some dressing and place them at the bottom of a plate.
7. Slice the beetroot into bite-sized pieces and place it on the lettuce.
8. Add the microgreens and roasted walnuts, and sprinkle over the roasted crumbled goat's cheese.
9. Top with the poached egg.

ORGANIC WHOLEGRAIN PASTA WITH PESTO

Pesto comes from the Genoese word *pestâ*, which means to crush. A simple, healthy meal that is hassle-free will become your go-to dish when you need to whip something up to impress.

SERVES 2

80 grams organic wholegrain fusilli or spaghetti
4 organic cherry tomatoes, halved
4 green beans, chopped
Parmesan, freshly grated

FOR THE PESTO

½ kilo basil
150 grams fresh parsley
200 grams fresh Parmesan
200 grams pine or cashew nuts
3 cloves garlic
3 cups extra virgin olive oil
Salt to taste

---

1. For the pesto, place the basil, parsley, Parmesan, nuts and garlic in a mortar and pestle and grind coarsely. Add a large pinch of salt while grinding.

   You can also do this in a blender if you're pressed for time.

2 Once the ingredients resemble a rough sauce, begin adding the olive oil and keep grinding. Choose a nice thick green olive oil to get additional flavour and texture.

3. Put a large pot of salted water to boil and add your pasta to it. Boil it for one minute less than the instructions on the packet.

4. Add the green beans 2 minutes before the end. Drain the pasta and beans and transfer them to a warm, greased frying pan.

5. Add a dollop of the freshly made pesto sauce and toss till everything is coated evenly.

6. Top with the cherry tomatoes and serve, garnished with grated Parmesan.

TAMOTA PAR EEDA

No meal in a Parsi house is complete without one egg or 'eeda' dish. Tamota par eeda is one of the most common things you will find at a Parsi dining table. This punchy, slightly sweet, slightly sour dish can be baked in an oven or cooked on a frying pan if you prefer.

SERVES 1

2 eggs
4 tomatoes, rough chopped
2 small onions, rough chopped
1 tablespoon ginger-garlic paste
½ teaspoon turmeric powder
1 green chilli, finely chopped
½ teaspoon sugar cane vinegar
A handful of fresh coriander leaves
Salt to taste

Preheat your oven to 180°C

1. Heat a little vegetable oil in a frying pan and add the onions.
2. Fry the onions until they are translucent and add the ginger-garlic paste, turmeric powder and salt. Stir well.
3. Add the chopped tomato and sugar cane vinegar and sauté for a few minutes, adding a handful of coriander leaves towards the end.
4. Grease a ramekin or small baking pot and fill it with the sautéed tomatoes.
5. Crack two eggs over the tomatoes and place the ramekin carefully in the oven. Cook until the eggs are done to the way you like – you can have the yolks runny or hard.
6. Garnish with some more fresh coriander and serve with toast.

ROCK SHRIMP LECHE DE TIGRE

Gently poached rock shrimp is accompanied by citrusy leche de tigre or Tiger's Milk, topped with red bell pepper gel, garnished with cucumber, orange and chilli and served cold with crisp prawn crackers.

SERVES 4

FOR THE LECHE DE TIGRE

650 ml coconut cream
1 yellow bell pepper, sliced
240 grams celery, sliced
10 cloves garlic, thinly sliced
24 grams ginger, thinly sliced
1½ teaspoons yellow chilli powder
60 grams lime juice
40 grams shiro dashi or white soy
0.6 grams xantham gum
Salt to taste

500 ml vegetable stock (page 132)
1 kg rock shrimp, with shells
1 orange, peeled, deseeded and diced
1 cucumber, seedless and diced
2 tablespoons red bell pepper gel (page132)
¼ cup Madras onions, rings
¼ cup corn kernels, blanched
2 red chillis, skin cut into slivers
A handful of coriander sprigs
Prawn crackers, fried
Salt to taste

---

1. Heat the vegetable stock on a gentle simmer for 20 minutes and then add your shrimp.
2. Allow the shrimp to cook until they begin to curl and quickly take them off the heat.
3. Cool them immediately in an ice bath to stop them from cooking.
4. Peel, de-vein and trim them into small pieces and refrigerate until serving.
5 To make the leche de tigre, mix the coconut cream, bell pepper, celery, garlic, ginger and chilli powder to a smooth liquid in a blender.
6. Strain through a sieve and add lime juice and shiro dashi, and season with salt.
7. Gently shear in the xantham gum in bits and mix well. Add as much as needed. Xantham gum is a thickening agent and a good substitute for cornflour.
8 Strain the sauce once again and keep refrigerated until you need it.
9. To assemble, dress the shrimp lightly with the leche de tigre and season with salt.
10. Place the shrimp in serving dishes and pour over the leche de tigre. Pipe drops of the red bell pepper gel to garnish.
11. Decorate with cucumber, orange, chilli, coriander, onion and corn.

BEETROOT RISOTTO

Creamy beetroot risotto with dill mascarpone is the ultimate exhibitionist. With its shocking pink colour and smooth undertones, this dish is simply sinful with every bite.

SERVES 2

FOR THE RISOTTO

- 4 tablespoons butter
- ½ cup leek, finely chopped
- 1 cup carnaroli rice
- 3 cups vegetable stock (page 132)
- 1 tablespoon beetroot purée
- 1 tablespoon beetroot dice
- ¼ cup Parmesan
- 2 tablespoons dill mascarpone (page 132)
- Salt to taste

FOR THE BEETROOT PURÉE AND DICE

- 500 grams beetroot
- ¼ cup olive oil
- 3 sprigs rosemary
- 5 sprigs thyme

Preheat your oven to 170°C

1. To make the beetroot purée and dice, place the beetroot, along with sprigs of rosemary and thyme on a baking sheet and bake uncovered for 45 minutes.
2. Put half the cooked beetroot into a blender and make a thick purée. Dice the rest of the beetroot into small cubes.
3. For the risotto, shallow cook the leek in 2 tablespoons of butter until it is soft and add the risotto rice to the pan. Stir the rice around for a few minutes until it is lightly toasted.
4. Add a ladle of vegetable stock to the rice and allow it to be absorbed.
5. Continue adding a ladle of stock each time until the stock is completely absorbed and the rice is cooked al dente.
6. Finish your risotto by adding the remaining butter, Parmesan, beetroot purée and diced beets.
7. Stir the risotto vigorously until it is creamy, with the consistency of a loose porridge.
8. Top the risotto with a dollop of dill mascarpone and garnish with a sprig of fresh dill.

SOM TAM SALAD

Green papaya salad is a fresh, happy and healthy choice for any dinner table. Addictively hot and refreshingly crunchy, this Thai staple has been called the world's best salad, time and time again.

SERVES 2

1	large green papaya
150	grams garlic, peeled
75	grams red chilli, finely sliced
150	grams jaggery
4	lemons, juiced
250	grams green beans, sliced
150	grams cherry tomatoes, halved
50	ml fish sauce
100	grams dried prawns
1	raw mango

1. Cut the green papaya and raw mango in shreds with a zigzag or som tam peeler and keep aside in an ice bath.
2. Take whole pieces of garlic and chilli and throw them into a mortar and pestle (preferably a som tam mortar and pestle). Grind until you have a rough paste.
3. Add the lemon juice and fish sauce and continue to grind.
4. Next add the beans, jaggery, cherry tomatoes and dried prawns and mix.
5. Lastly, add the green papaya and raw mango and bring the salad together with a spoon.
6. Taste and serve with a garnish of Thai basil, crushed peanuts and mint.

GOI CUON

Also known as Vietnamese summer rolls, *goi cuon* are fresh pickled vegetables wrapped in rice paper. They make a great appetizer that is perfect for an Asian inspired meal.

SERVES 2

4	pieces Vietnamese rice paper - *Banh Trang*
50	grams white radish, julienned
50	grams red carrots, julienned
50	grams fresh cucumber, julienned
60	grams tofu, julienned
200	ml sugar syrup
200	ml vinegar
½	bunch coriander
½	bunch mint
½	bunch basil
½	iceberg lettuce

1. Mix the vinegar and the sugar syrup and refrigerate for one hour.
2. Place the sliced radish, cucumber, carrot and tofu in a glass bowl and pour the syrup mixture over it. Refrigerate for at least 4 hours or overnight to allow the vegetables to pickle.
3. Wash the coriander, basil, mint and iceberg lettuce properly and separate into individual pieces. Pat dry and keep aside.
4. Wet a clean kitchen cloth and place it on a chopping board. Fill a *thali* with warm water and place the rice paper in it for a few seconds. Remove the paper from the *thali* and place it on the wet kitchen cloth. This allows the rice paper to become pliable.
5. Arrange your vegetables together on the bottom of the rice paper and start rolling them upwards like a sausage. Fold the rice paper in from the left and right side and continue rolling until you get to the end.
6. Cut the roll into bite-sized pieces and serve with sweet chilli sauce.

JAPANESE PRAWN TEMPURA

An ultra light batter that becomes crisp and golden goes perfectly with prawns for a light snack. Using sparkling water helps make the batter even lighter and the prawns ever crunchier.

SERVES 6

1 kg prawns IQF (individually quick frozen)
2-3 litres vegetable oil

FOR THE BATTER

500 grams cornflour
150 grams baking powder
150 ml water
8-10 ice cubes
4 eggs
Salt and pepper to taste

FOR THE TEMPURA SAUCE

60 ml light soya sauce
50 grams ginger, julienned
15 ml Mirin (Japanese rice wine)
Salt and sugar to taste

1. Beat your eggs until they are smooth and sift in the cornflour and baking powder. Keep mixing, adding the ice cubes and water slowly until you get a batter that is smooth and not thick.
2. Add salt and pepper to taste.
3. Heat the vegetable oil in a wok until the oil is smoking hot.
4. Dip each prawn into the batter, coating them evenly.
5. Add the prawns to the hot oil and fry each until they are a light golden colour.
6. Remove them with a slotted spoon and put on kitchen paper for a few minutes.
7. Mix the soya sauce, ginger and Mirin together to create a light sauce.
8. Serve together for a great tempura experience.

LOBSTER BISQUE

A smooth creamy bisque that embodies the taste of the sea, you can almost hear the sound of waves crashing on the shore with every spoonful.

SERVES 4

1½	kilos lobster heads
3	small onions, rough chopped
12	cloves garlic, rough chopped
1	carrot, rough chopped
1	litre water
2	tablespoons all-purpose flour
30	grams celery, rough chopped
100	ml brandy
500	ml cream
100	grams butter
400	grams tomato purée

1. Clean and roast the lobster heads in a pre-heated oven until they are bright orange in colour.
2. Sauté the onion, garlic, carrot and celery with butter in a thick-bottom pan till light brown.
3. Crush the lobster bones into small pieces using a wooden spoon. Add the crushed bones to the onions and sauté for 10 to 15 minutes.
4. Flambé the mixture with brandy. Breathe deeply!
5. Sprinkle a handful of flour over the lobster mixture and cook it until the flour becomes light brown.
6. Add the tomato purée and cook for another 10 minutes.
7. Then add a litre of water and simmer the soup for 5 to 6 hours on a very slow flame, removing the froth and impurities that rise to the surface at regular intervals.
8. Just before you are ready to serve, place the fresh cream in a saucepan on a slow flame and reduce to half the quantity.
9. Strain the lobster reduction through a fine strainer or muslin cloth and finish with the reduced fresh cream.
10. Season it with salt and pepper and then pass it through a double strainer once again for maximum gloss and smoothness.

CORN CRÊPE RAVIOLO

A twist on traditional ravioli, satiny corn crêpes form the base for a deliciously infused lemon grass cream, tofu and bok choy. This is vegetarian decadence at its best.

SERVES 4

250	grams corn *atta*
100	grams all-purpose flour
2	eggs
100	ml milk
200	grams tofu, cubed
800	grams bok choy, blanched
30	grams sambal olek
4	cloves garlic, rough chopped
150	grams spring onion, chopped
80	grams peanuts, boiled and peeled
3	bundles of lemon grass
500	ml cream
800	ml coconut milk
200	ml olive oil
	A pinch of nutmeg powder
	A handful of fresh chives

Preheat your oven to 175°C

1. Mix the corn *atta*, flour, eggs, milk, water and chives together in a bowl to make the crêpe batter. Season it with salt and pepper.
2. To make the crêpes, gently heat a non-stick pan and lightly grease it with butter. Spoon the batter onto the pan and spread it out thinly. Allow it to cook on a very low flame – you will know the crêpes are done when bubbles begin to form. Cut the crêpes into round shapes about 5 inches in diameter.
3. On a low flame, combine the cream with 3 bundles of lemon grass and reduce till you get a very aromatic lemon grass cream.
4. Add in the sambal olek, coconut milk, and nutmeg and season it with salt and pepper. Do not boil the sauce once the coconut milk is added. Pass it through a fine strainer to remove any lumps.
5. In a heavy-bottomed pan, sauté the chopped onion and garlic till golden brown. Add the bok choy, tofu and peanuts and sauté further.
6. Add a little of the lemon grass cream and let it simmer for 2 minutes. Season it with salt, pepper and chopped chives.
7. To assemble, place one of the crêpes on the bottom of a pasta bowl. Spoon the bok choy, tofu and peanut mixture in the middle and cover with another crêpe.
8. Pour the rest of the lemon grass cream over the crêpe and garnish with bell pepper salad and spring onion julienne.

GRAND MARNIER SOUFFLÉ

An airy concoction of egg whites is delicately flavoured with hints of tropical orange and fine cognac. A wonderful way to show your Valentine that you care.

SERVES 4

- 300 ml milk
- 4 egg yolks
- 40 grams granulated sugar
- 50 grams all-purpose flour
- 6 egg whites
- 110 grams castor sugar
- 60 ml Grand Marnier liquor

Preheat your oven to 175°C

Grease and prepare 4 ramekins with butter.

1. Whisk together the egg yolks, granulated sugar and flour.
2. Bring your milk to a boil in a saucepan and allow it to cool for a few minutes before pouring it over the egg yolk mixture a little at a time. Be careful not to add boiling milk as it might scramble the eggs.
3. Put your milk and egg mixture into another saucepan and cook it over a slow fire, mixing continuously with a whisk until you get a custard-like consistency.
4. Take the mixture off the heat and transfer it to a bowl, mixing in the Grand Marnier and whisking it well to ensure that there are no lumps.
5. In a separate bowl whip the egg whites with an electric beater until they are stiff and add in the castor sugar slowly, whipping continuously until all the sugar is added and there are soft peaks.
6. Gently fold the whipped egg whites into the custard, taking it one spoon at a time so as not to let the air escape. Do this slowly or the mixture will collapse and the soufflé will not rise.
7. Fill your ramekins with the soufflé custard and bake them for 8 to 10 minutes.
8. Remove the soufflés from the oven and serve immediately, with stewed strawberries and fresh cream on the side.

Times Kala Ghoda Arts
WESTSIDE
Nutrela
WESTSIDE

AT THE KALA GHODA ARTS FESTIVAL

BOK CHOY RAMEN SALAD

A homemade vinaigrette perfectly accentuates the freshness of green bok choy and crunchy noodles, topped with almond slivers and spring onion.

SERVES 4

250 grams chopped bok choy
100 grams almond slivers, toasted
80 grams spring onions
1 packet dry instant noodles
2 tablespoons brown sugar
4 tablespoons vinegar
4 tablespoons peanut oil
1 tablespoon soya sauce
1 tablespoon sesame oil

Preheat your oven to 180°C

1. To clean the bok choy, remove the choke from the bottom of the stem with the help of a turning knife. Thinly slice the bok choy and cut the spring onion stalks in julienne.
2. Wash the leaves thoroughly and dry them with the help of a salad spinner.
3. To make the dressing, whisk the brown sugar, vinegar, soya sauce, sesame oil and peanut oil together in a bowl.
4. Toast your noodles in a preheated oven for 3 to 4 minutes, until they have become golden brown.
5. Mix the bok choy leaves with the dressing. Garnish with crispy noodles and almond slivers and serve.

CANDIED PUMPKIN SOUP

A fun twist on traditional *bhopla*, this soup brings out the sweetness of pumkin as it slowly caramelises – 'candies' – and will have your kids eating their vegetables and loving them too.

SERVES 4

- 750 grams pumpkin, cubed
- 150 grams cream
- 150 ml milk
- 1 tablespoon oil
- 1½ cups water
- 1 teaspoon salt
- 1 teaspoon pepper
- 4 cloves garlic, rough chopped
- 3 tablespoons honey
- ¼ cup lemon juice
- A handful of parsley

---

1. Peel and dice the pumpkin into cubes, approximately 1.5 cm in size.
2. Heat the oil on a non-stick pan and add the garlic and diced pumpkin. Sauté until the pumpkin is golden brown.
3. Turn down the heat and add water, cream and milk. Allow it to come to a boil. Turn the heat down lower and simmer for another 5 minutes.
4. Add salt and pepper.
5. Transfer the hot pumpkin mix to a blender and mix until smooth.
6. Finish the soup with honey, lemon juice and parsley, adjusting the seasoning as needed.
7. Serve hot topped with a drizzle of olive oil.

MUSHROOM GNOCCHI

Warm mushroom sauce is the perfect companion for fluffy potato gnocci.

SERVES 6

FOR THE GNOCCHI

1½	kilos potatoes
250	grams refined flour
125	grams Parmesan, grated
½	teaspoon nutmeg powder
1	teaspoon salt

FOR THE SAUCE

250	grams button mushrooms, sliced
1½	teaspoons salt
1	teaspoon cracked pepper
25	ml cream
1	tablespoon vegetable oil
¼	cup water

Preheat your oven to 180°C

1. While making gnocchi, be sure to choose standard potatoes.

Score the potatoes with a knife and roast them in a preheated oven for 1½ hours. They are cooked when you can smoothly insert a toothpick or paring knife.

2. Scoop out the insides of the potatoes and mash them while they're still hot. Allow the mixture to cool.

3. Combine the potato mash, nutmeg, salt, refined flour and Parmesan in a large mixing bowl. Gently mash the mix with your hands to form the dough.

4. Roll the dough into small balls about 1 cm in diameter – the gnocchi should resemble small marbles. With the back of a spoon, gently press the tops so that they flatten slightly.

5. Bring a big pan of salted water to boil and cook the gnocchi in small batches. They are done when they float on the water's surface. Remove them with a slotted spoon and place them on a cooling tray.

6. To make the mushroom sauce, sauté the sliced mushrooms in small batches on a smoking hot pan with 1 teaspoon of oil for about 2 minutes.

8. Leaving a handful of mushroom quarters aside, put the rest into a blender with hot water. Season the purée with salt and pepper and allow it to cool before proceeding.

9. Gently fold cream into your mushroom purée to complete your sauce.

10. To serve the gnocchi, heat a teaspoon of olive oil in a non-stick pan and toss the gnocchi along with the mushroom quarters until golden brown.

11. Finish off with the mushroom sauce.

APPLE WOOD-SMOKED BARBECUE CHICKEN

This barbeque dish is packed full of flavour. Succulent chicken with a smoky char is topped with toasted sesame seeds and spring onion greens.

SERVES 2

200 grams boneless chicken legs
5 cloves garlic, chopped
5 Kashmiri red chillis, chopped
2 pieces star anise, crushed
10 ml oyster sauce
1 tablespoon soya sauce
1 teaspoon ginger juice
1 tablespoon Sriracha or any other hot sauce
5 basil leaves, rough chopped
Salt and pepper to taste

FOR THE MARINADE

1 tablespoon oyster sauce
1¾ tablespoons soya sauce
3½ tablespoons barbecue sauce

1 teaspoon white sesame seeds, toasted
1 teaspoon black sesame seeds, toasted
1 handful of spring onion greens, chopped

---

1. Mix the oyster sauce, soya sauce and barbecue sauce together in a bowl.
2. Clean the chicken and marinate it in half the sauce mixture for at least 30 minutes.
3. If you are able to access a charcoal barbecue, now is a good time to get it going. Otherwise place a cast iron griddle pan on a high flame and allow it to get smoking hot.
4. Prepare your sauce for grilling. In a large bowl, mix the chopped garlic, chilli, basil and star anise with the rest of the sauces and ginger juice. Season with salt and pepper.
5. Grill the chicken, continuously basting it with the grilling sauce and marinade to make sure it does not dry out. This should take about 7 to 8 minutes.
6. Heat a few small pieces of charcoal and place them with a handful of apple wood chips at the edge of a platter. Make sure the wood chips catch and are smoking. Alternatively place apple wood chips into a smoking gun.
7. Quickly put the cooked chicken pieces onto the platter with the wood chips and charcoal and cover with a dome. Allow the chicken to absorb the smoky barbecue flavour of the apple wood chips.
8. Sprinkle with toasted black and white sesame seeds and some spring onion. Serve with a flourish!

KHOWSUEY

A Burmese dish that needs no introduction, this is the consummate 'do it yourself' meal. A curry served with noodles and an array of condiments allows everyone to tailor the flavours of the meal to suit themselves.

SERVES 6

FOR THE PASTE

25	grams ginger
25	grams garlic
50	grams Kashmiri red chilli
1	tablespoon turmeric powder

FOR THE SOUP

50	grams *khowsuey* paste
1	tablespoon oil
20	grams celery, chopped
10	grams lemon grass, chopped
½	cup water
1	litre vegetable stock (page 132)
2	tablespoons vegetable oyster sauce
1	teaspoon turmeric powder
500	ml coconut milk

ACCOMPANIMENTS

50	grams steamed noodles
20	grams fried noodles
20	grams burnt garlic, finely chopped
20	grams spring onion, chopped
20	grams fried onion, finely chopped
20	ml chilli vinegar
1	wedge of lime

---

1. Dry roast the ginger, garlic, red chilli and turmeric in a pan. Once the garlic and ginger change colour, transfer everything to a mortar and pestle and grind into a thick paste.

2. Add some oil to a frying pan on a medium flame and gently fry the paste. Use a few tablespoons of water as you fry it, being careful not to burn it. Add the turmeric and allow it to cook with the paste. Tie the lemon grass and celery together to form a bouquet garni and add it to the paste. Fry for 1 minute before adding the oyster sauce, half the vegetable stock and a third of the coconut milk.

3. Mix well and allow it to come to a simmer. Keep in mind that you need to skim the scum released through the oil off the top of the soup as it simmers.

4. Adjust the consistency of the soup with the remaining coconut milk and vegetable stock. Add them a tablespoon at a time to thicken. You do not need to use all the stock and milk, and can stop when you are comfortable with the soup.

5. Place your steamed noodles in a wide bowl and pour the piping hot *khowsuey* through a strainer. If you'd like to add chicken or prawn, add 100 grams of steamed prawn or chicken to the bowl and pour the *khowsuey* over it.

Garnish with chopped spring onion.

7. Serve on a large platter along with small bowls of fried noodles, burnt garlic, fried onion, spring onion and a wedge of lime.

FILO MILLE FEUILLE

Fluffy crème Chantilly and berries are pressed between airy, crispy and flaky filo sheets and combines to form a decadent dessert that takes almost no time at all to make and is a must-have in your culinary artillery.

SERVES 2

10 sheets frozen filo pastry
5 tablespoons melted butter

FOR THE CHANTILLY CREAM

300 grams mascarpone cream
100 grams whipped cream
12 grams gelatin
75 grams sugar
20 ml honey
50 grams blueberries
50 grams cranberries
50 grams blackberries
25 grams sugar
45 ml water

Preheat your oven to 200°C

1. Brush the edges of 2 sheets of filo pastry with melted butter and stick them together. Repeat this process until you have 5 double sheets.
2. Cut each sheet into rectangles that are roughly 3 cm x 4 cm in dimension and place on a baking sheet. Bake them until they are puffy and golden brown and set aside to cool.
3. Dissolve the gelatin in warm water. Fold the whipped cream into the mascarpone in a mixing bowl. Add the sugar slowly and incorporate.
4. Stir in the gelatin and honey and mix. Refrigerate until it has set slightly.
5. To make your berry mix, put the blackberries, cranberries and blueberries into another bowl and add the sugar and water. Stir well and allow the juices to come together.
6. To assemble, spoon the crème Chantilly into a piping bag with a narrow nozzle. Pipe a small blob onto the centre of a funky plate. Place a rectangle of filo pastry onto the cream and press down lightly. This prevents the pastry from slipping all over the plate.
7. Pipe cream along the edges of the filo pastry and spoon berries into the centre. Place another piece of filo on top and repeat the process.
8. Repeat this process for 4 layers of filo pastry and garnish with some cream and blueberry sauce.
9. This makes one Mille Feuille. Repeat with glee for the second. Perfect for sharing with friends.

BEETROOT KEFTEDES

Serve these Greek-influenced beetroot fritters with mezze, eat them hot in pita with salad or keep them in the fridge for an easy lunch.

SERVES 4

120 grams beetroot
30 grams feta cheese
1 teaspoon dill, rough chopped
1 tablespoon parsley, rough chopped
1 tablespoon Parmesan, grated
30 grams breadcrumbs
10 ml cooking oil
Salt and pepper to taste

---

1. Boil the beetroot until you can easily slide a knife through it. Once it has cooled, remove the skin and grate it. Using a muslin cloth, squeeze the liquid out of the grated beetroot until it is almost dry.
2. Add the grated beetroot, chopped dill, chopped parsley, Parmesan, breadcrumbs, feta cheese, salt and pepper in a mixing bowl and combine.
3. Make small roundels in the palm of your hand. You should have approximately 10 *keftedes* from the mixture.
4. Sear the *keftedes* on a non-stick pan with a little oil until the outsides are crispy.
5. Serve hot with some tzatziki.

BROWN RICE PAELLA

Whole grain brown rice is accompanied by broad beans, olives, grilled artichokes, roasted fennel and peppers. Add pieces of grilled chicken or prawns to give it a carnivorous twist.

SERVES 2

50	grams brown rice
100	ml tomato concasse (page 132)
250	ml vegetable stock (page 132)
250	ml white wine
50	grams onion, rough chopped
50	ml olive oil
50	grams fennel bulb
½	teaspoon chilli flakes
4	cloves garlic, chopped
50	grams red and yellow bell pepper, diced
5	olives
10	broad beans
2	artichokes
	A handful of fresh basil leaves, chopped
	Salt and pepper to taste

1. In a wide-bottom saucepan, sauté the onion and garlic in olive oil. Add the chilli flakes and continue to sauté.
2. Add the brown rice and cook until it becomes transparent.
3. Add a splash of white wine and continue to cook till the wine evaporates.
4. Follow this with a ladle of vegetable stock and continue to cook till that evaporates.
5. Repeat the process of a ladle of wine followed by a ladle of stock until you have almost finished the stock or you think that the rice is almost cooked through.
6. Add the basil at any point while cooking the rice.
7. Add the tomato concasse and continue cooking until the rice is done. Keep in mind that brown rice takes a lot longer to cook than white rice, and will use more liquid. Season with salt and pepper.
8. In another pan, sauté the red and yellow bell peppers, fennel, broad beans, artichoke and olives.
9. Season with salt, pepper and parsley.
10. To serve, put the paella in a serving dish and top with the sautéed vegetables.

SPAGHETTI WITH GARDEN VEGETABLES

A bounty from the garden makes a delicious fresh pasta that is the perfect dish for summer lunches.

SERVES 2

150	grams spaghetti
50	grams baby corn, sliced lengthwise
50	grams green beans
1	clove garlic, chopped
½	teaspoon chilli flakes
10	grams sun-dried tomatoes
1	teaspoon capers
4	broccoli florets
1	tablespoon garlic breadcrumbs
1	tablespoon Parmesan, grated
30	ml olive oil
	A handful of fresh basil leaves, chopped
	Salt and pepper to taste

1. Set a pot of water to boil and cook your pasta as per the instructions on the package. Try and keep the spaghetti 'al dente' – it should still have a little bite to it at the end.
2. Blanch all your vegetables in boiling hot water i.e. dip the vegetables in boiling water for a few minutes. This is enough to begin cooking, but will not cause the vegetables to become soggy and lose their shape.
3. Heat the olive oil in a pan, and add chopped garlic and chilli flakes to sauté.
4. Add the blanched vegetables to the pan, along with the olives, sun-dried tomatoes, capers and the cooked, drained pasta.
5. Toss well and make sure everything is coated evenly. Add the garlic breadcrumbs and season with salt and pepper to taste.
6. Sprinkle grated Parmesan over the spaghetti and serve.

STICKY TOFFEE PUDDING

A rich, moist cake dotted with dates is permeated with a thick caramel-like sauce and topped with candied ginger, causing delight with every mouthful.

SERVES 4

FOR THE PUDDING

225 grams pitted dates
175 grams all-purpose flour
85 grams butter
100 ml milk
175 ml orange juice
140 grams brown sugar
2 eggs
1 teaspoon baking soda

FOR THE TOFFEE

600 grams brown sugar
300 grams cream
100 ml milk
150 grams butter

Preheat your oven to 160°C

Prepare 6 ramekins by lining them with baking paper or buttering and flouring the bottom and sides.

1. To make the pudding, bring the orange juice up to the boil and add the pitted dates to it. Let it rest until it comes down to room temperature.
2. In a separate bowl, cream the butter and sugar together until pale and fluffy.
3. Add the eggs to the butter and sugar one at a time, followed by the flour in 3 parts.
4. Make sure the date mixture has cooled down – you don't want to scramble the eggs! Add the date mixture and milk to the eggs and mix well.
5. Divide the mixture into your ramekins and place them in a large baking tray. Pour boiling water halfway up the sides and place the tray into your preheated oven.
6. Bake the ramekins for 20 to 25 minutes. You will know they are done when you insert a toothpick or sharp knife into the centre and it comes out clean.
7. Allow the puddings to rest once they have come out of the oven.
8. For the sauce, melt the butter and sugar together over a low flame until it caramelizes and turns honey brown.
9. Slowly add the milk and cream, continuously stirring. This will come together to make a smooth, sticky sauce that can be poured all over the pudding.
10. Carefully remove each pudding from its ramekin when cool, and place on individual flat plates.
11. Pour a generous amount of the toffee sauce over each pudding and serve with ice cream.

BROWNIE DULCHE DE LECHE

These rich, fudgy brownies run through with decadent dulche de leche are a sinful treat to be enjoyed on any day.

SERVES 4

- 200 grams 70% dark chocolate
- 100 grams butter
- 100 grams sugar
- 2 eggs
- 60 grams all-purpose flour
- 50 ml water
- 50 grams dulce de leche

Preheat your oven to 200°C

Prepare a square baking dish by lining it with baking paper or buttering and flouring the bottom and sides.

1. Melt the chocolate and butter together over a low flame. Add the sugar and mix well.
2. Remove the mixture from the heat and add water. Stir until combined.
3. Making sure that the mixture has cooled, add the eggs one at a time and mix well.
4. Fold in the flour.

   Pour in half the mixture and refrigerate for 1½ hours.
5. Pour the dulce de leche mixture evenly over the chilled brownie batter and put it back into the fridge for 20 mins.
6. Pour the rest of the brownie batter on top of the set mix and put into your preheated oven.
7. Bake the brownies for 15 to 20 minutes. Cut them into squares and serve warm.

CHOCOLATE SALTED CARAMEL TART

Nothing says 'I love you' quite like this buttery chocolate pastry with a rich chocolate and caramel ganache brought together in the ultimate marriage of flavours.

SERVES 8

FOR THE GANACHE

200 grams 70% dark chocolate
240 grams salted butter
180 ml cream
80 grams sugar
80 ml water

FOR THE TART

100 grams all-purpose flour
70 grams butter
40 grams icing sugar
1 tablespoon cocoa powder
14 ml milk

Preheat your oven to 180°C

Butter and flour 6 mini tart pans or 1 large 9-inch tart pan.

1. Mix the flour, sugar and cocoa powder together. Rub the butter and flour together with your fingers until the mixture looks like coarse breadcrumbs.
2. Add the milk and gently press the dough until it comes together.
3. Wrap the dough in cling wrap and chill it for 30 minutes. This will help the dough hold its elasticity.
4. Take the dough out of the fridge and roll it out on a well floured surface. Roll the pastry out to 4 mm thickness. The dough is extremely light and flaky, be careful not to press too hard.
5. Cut the dough into circles that are slightly bigger than your tart dish and gently place the dough into it. Press it down and up against the sides carefully and place in the fridge for another ten minutes.
6. Prick the base all over with a fork and bake it for 12 to 15 minutes.
7. To make the ganache, boil the water, sugar and cream together in a heavy-bottomed saucepan over a low flame.
8. Remove the saucepan from the heat and add the chocolate into it. Swirl it around and allow it to melt.
9. Add the butter to the chocolate and mix until combined.
10. Pour the ganache into the baked tart base and chill for at least 3 hours.

Garnish with fresh raspberries, chocolate shards or praline.

HALEEM

It is said that once you have had a taste of haleem, you never forget it. The slow cooked richness of the meat is enhanced by barley, lentils, wheat and an array of spices; each adding its own depth to the dish.

SERVES 2

½ cup ghee
1 cinnamon stick
4 cloves
3 green cardamom pods
2 bay leaves
120 grams onion, thinly sliced
1 tablespoon ginger-garlic paste
30 grams (raw) soaked lapsi
150 grams boneless mutton leg
1½ cups curd
2 teaspoons whole coriander
½ teaspoon yellow chilli powder
1 teaspoon rose water
20 grams cashew nut paste
½ a bunch of mint leaves
1 gram saffron water, mixed in 30 ml warm milk
2 cups mutton stock
½ a bunch of fresh coriander leaves

½ cup onion, fried
A pinch of rose petals
A few strings of khus ki jhad
Salt and pepper to taste

---

1. In a wide heavy-bottomed pan heat a few tablespoons of ghee and add half the sliced onion. Sauté until the onion is translucent and add the ginger-garlic paste.
2. Cut the boneless mutton leg into ½ cm cubes and add them to the pan. Sauté the mutton for a minute or so, until it begins to brown.
3. Add the *lapsi* to the sautéed mutton and pour in both cups of stock.
4. Make a bouquet garni with the cinnamon stick, rose petals, coriander, cloves, green cardamom, bay leaf, *khus ki jhad* and add to the pan. Cover with a lid and cook on a medium flame till the mutton becomes tender.
5. Add the curd, yellow chilli powder, black pepper powder, cashew nut paste, rose water, saffron water, salt to taste and cook until the mutton has softened into a paste. Don't be impatient, the longer you cook the haleem, the softer and smoother it becomes.
6. Serve hot with chopped mint and coriander, a few fried cashew nuts, a generous sprinkling of fried onion and a dollop of ghee.

MALPUA

Malpua is just what you need to warm your heart on a cold winter day. The smell of the sugary, spicy batter gently cooking in ghee with wafts of saffron drifting by has made this dish one of India's most popular desserts.

SERVES 2

FOR THE MALPUA BATTER

100 grams plain white *mawa*, grated
100 ml milk
2 ml saffron water
2½ tablespoons refined flour
1½ teaspoons cornflour
A pinch or two of green cardamom powder

FOR THE SUGAR SYRUP

100 grams granulated sugar
150 ml water
½ teaspoon saffron water

2 grams pistachios, sliced
2 grams almonds, sliced
Ghee

1. In a heavy-bottomed saucepan, bring the milk to a boil. Gently whisk in the grated *mawa* until it dissolves. Allow it to cool slightly.
2. Add the cornflour and refined flour to the milk, whisking gently, one tablespoon at a time. Continue mixing until both flours are dissolved and the mixture is smooth.
3. Sprinkle a pinch or two of green cardamom powder and the saffron water into the mixture. Your batter for the malpua is now ready.
4. To make your sugar syrup, dissolve sugar and water in a small saucepan and heat until a syrupy consistency is achieved.
5. Remove the syrup from the flame and add 3 ml saffron water to it. Stir gently and cover to keep warm.
6. Heat ghee in a pan on a low flame, and carefully pour your batter onto it, one ladle at a time. You should make small flat round discs, a little smaller than a saucer. Fry each until golden brown.
7. Dip the fried malpua into the warm sugar syrup for 1 to 2 minutes, and then place on a flat plate.
8. Drizzle with some syrup and garnish with thinly sliced almond and pistachio.

PARDE ME KHUBANI

Also known as apricot *halwa*, this dessert is unapologetic decadence. Eat through your guilt because the buttery pastry and subtly sweet apricot filling is what cheat days are made for.

SERVES 4

600 grams apricot
140 grams brown *mawa*, grated
100 ml ghee
4 tablespoons castor sugar
½ teaspoon green cardamom powder
2 teaspoons saffron water
2 sheets puff pastry

Soak the apricots in water for at least 12 hours and de-seed.

When you are ready to start, preheat your oven to 200°C.

Prepare 6 ramekins by lining them with baking paper or buttering and flouring the bottom and sides.

1. Cook the apricots on a low flame for 15 to 20 minutes, mashing continuously until the flesh softens.
2. Add the grated *mawa* and stir. Cook the apricots and *mawa* for 12 to 15 minutes, stirring continuously until they are well mixed.
3. Pour ghee into the saucepan and continue cooking for another 10 to 12 minutes until the mixture gets a nice shiny gloss.
4. Fold in the castor sugar and cook until it has blended into the mixture. Sprinkle green cardamom powder and saffron water and cook for another 2 minutes.
5. Cut your puff pastry into rounds that are slightly bigger than your ramekins. You will need the pastry to overlap in order to make a complete cover.
6. Divide the mixture into ramekins and cover them with a thick layer of puff pastry. Stick the pastry to the outer sides of the ramekin with a little butter.
7. Bake in a preheated oven for about 7 to 8 minutes and serve immediately.

MUSHROOM TEA

This clear broth is full of earthy flavour and is a delightful way to serve mushroom consommé and surprise your guests.

SERVES 4

100 grams dry shiitake mushrooms, rough chopped
100 grams fresh button mushrooms, rough chopped
80 grams leek, rough chopped
30 grams garlic
50 grams white onion
2 litres water
1 teaspoon whole black pepper
A few sprigs of parsley
Salt to taste

1. Wash and cut the mushrooms and leek into large pieces.
2. Peel and cut the onions into quarters.
3. Place the button mushrooms, leek, garlic, onion, parsley and pepper in a large stockpot and bring it to a gentle boil.
4. Turn down the heat after 20 minutes and allow it to simmer for another 20 minutes.
5. Add the shiitake mushrooms and cook on a very low flame, so that there are no bubbles – this prevents the stock from getting cloudy.
6. Continue cooking on a low flame until it has reduced to about half. This could take anywhere between 30 and 45 minutes.
7. Strain the tea through a sieve and discard the solid ingredients.
8. Add some salt to taste, chopped parsley and a few tiny bits of the shiitake mushroom.

   For a fun twist, serve this hot in teacups.

GAMBAS AL AJILLO

Gambas al ajillo is a quick and easy dish that is packed with a punch. Its flavourful broth begs to be soaked up with crunchy, crusty bread long after you have finished eating every prawn.

SERVES 2

120 grams large prawns, deveined with head on
80 ml fish stock (page 132)
20 ml extra virgin olive oil
10 grams garlic, thinly sliced into flakes
50 grams butter
1½ teaspoons chilli flakes
A handful of fresh coriander leaves
Salt to taste

1. Place a heavy-bottomed pan over high heat and allow it to get smoking hot.
2. Once the pan is extremely hot, pour in the olive oil followed by the garlic and chilli flakes.
3. Add the prawns and instantly add the fish stock. Allow it to simmer for 1 minute.
4. Add the butter and coriander leaves and take off the flame.
5. Serve in a pasta plate, with warm crusty bread.

POMEGRANATE MOLASSES SALMON

A citrusy twist to a fillet of salmon marinated in ruby red pomegranate molasses and topped with dill sour cream, asparagus and radish.

SERVES 2

2	fillets of salmon, approximately 120 – 150 grams each
1	litre pomegranate juice
50	grams sour cream
8	asparagus stalks
2	red radish, finely sliced
½	teaspoon salt
	A handful of dill leaves, chopped

Preheat your oven to 220°C

1. To make the pomegranate molasses, place the pomegranate juice in a deep saucepan on a medium flame and reduce the liquid until it is thick and sticky, and around 100 ml.
2. To clean the asparagus, peel the bottom of each stalk and break off the hard bits. Blanch the asparagus by placing the stalks in a pot of boiling salted water for 1 minute and transfer them into a bowl of ice-cold water immediately. This stops the asparagus from cooking further. Set aside.
3. Mix your chopped dill with the sour cream and whisk until blended.
4. Sprinkle salt over the salmon. Spread the reduced pomegranate molasses on each piece with a brush, allowing for a thick gloopy layer of bright red.
5. Place the fish on a layer of foil and grill in the oven uncovered for 6 minutes. After 3 minutes, place the asparagus on the same tray and allow it to bake with the salmon fillets.
6. Remove the fish from the oven and plate it with radish and the sour cream.
7. Add the asparagus to each plate and serve.

PORTUGUESE ROAST CHICKEN

Smoky, spicy Portuguese roast chicken is accompanied by piri piri rice and sauce, making it a perfect meal for the whole family.

SERVES 4

FOR THE CHICKEN

1	whole chicken
¼	cup fresh lime juice
1½	tablespoons olive oil
2	cloves garlic, crushed
1	teaspoon chilli flakes
1	teaspoon salt
1	teaspoon ground coriander
½	teaspoon sweet paprika
½	teaspoon dried oregano
½	cup piri piri sauce (page 132)

FOR THE RICE

1½	cups long-grain white rice
1½	cups onion, finely chopped
1½	cups tomatoes, chopped
2	teaspoons garlic, minced
2	tablespoons fresh parsley, chopped
2	tablespoons fresh coriander, chopped
½	teaspoon chilli flakes, crushed
2¼	cups water
¼	cup olive oil
1½	teaspoons salt
1	bay leaf

---

1. Cut the chicken down its breastbone and open flat. Remove and discard the backbone by cutting on either side. Alternatively, have your butcher do this and save yourself the hassle.
2. Whisk the lime juice, olive oil, garlic, chilli flakes, salt, coriander, paprika and oregano together in a bowl.
3. Pour the marinade over the chicken and refrigerate it for 2 hours.
4. Preheat your oven to 200°C.
5. Put the chicken on a roasting tray, and baste it with the marinade once more. Cook for 50 minutes or until it is golden and cooked through.
6. While the chicken is cooking, heat the oil over high heat in a deep saucepan until hot.
7. Add the onion to the pan and sauté until it has softened, which should take about 4 minutes.
8. Add the garlic, salt, chilli flakes and bay leaf and stir for 1 minute. Follow this with your tomatoes, still stirring for another 2 minutes.
9. Add the rice, water, parsley and coriander and bring it to a boil. Cook the rice undisturbed for 20 minutes until the liquid is dissolved and the rice is tender.
10. Let the rice stand for 5 minutes undisturbed before fluffing it with a fork.
11. Serve immediately with the chicken and piri piri sauce.

THAI FISH CAKES

Fish cakes are a common street food in Thailand and pack a whole lot of flavour. Drawing inspiration from traditional red Thai curry, these little morsels are accompanied with sweet and spicy pineapple chutney.

SERVES 4

FOR THE FISH CAKES

500 grams fish fillets and trimmings
1 teaspoon lime leaf, julienned
1 teaspoon lemon grass, finely chopped
1 teaspoon red curry paste
⅓ cup green beans, finely chopped
½ teaspoon fish sauce
1 teaspoon coriander leaves
1 teaspoon lime juice
1 egg yolk
1 cup breadcrumbs
1-2 litres vegetable oil
A pinch of white pepper

FOR THE PINEAPPLE CHUTNEY

150 grams pineapple, finely diced
50 grams sugar
40 ml white vinegar
½ teaspoon chilli flakes
1 cinnamon stick
2 lime leaves
1 small stalk lemon grass
1 teaspoon garlic, finely chopped
⅓ cup spring onion, chopped
1 teaspoon coriander leaves, chopped

1. To make the chutney, add sugar and vinegar in a pot and reduce it by half on a medium flame.
2. Add the pineapple, chilli flakes, cinnamon stick, lime leaves, lemon grass and garlic to the syrup and cook until the pineapple softens and most of the liquid evaporates.
3. Take it off the heat and add the chopped spring onion and coriander leaves.
4. For the fish cakes, place the fish in a food processor along with the lime leaf, lemon grass, curry paste, green beans, fish sauce, coriander, lime juice and egg yolk.
5. Blend together until you get a thick paste. Avoid mixing the ingredients too much or the texture of the fish cakes will become rubbery. You can also mix the ingredients together by hand.
6. Shape the fish mixture into balls in the palm of your hand. Press down with one palm and flatten them into cakes.
7. Scatter breadcrumbs on a plate and place the fish cakes on them. Cover the fish cakes evenly with breadcrumbs.
8. Heat some oil in a heavy-bottomed pan and deep-fry the fish cakes until they are golden brown.
9. Place them on a paper towel to drain and serve with pineapple chutney and fresh salad.

MILK CHOCOLATE AND HAZELNUT TRUFFLES

These eggless delights are easy to make and will have your friend's eyes opening in wonder. It's best to make these in the morning or the evening when it's not too hot in your kitchen.

SERVES 4

300 grams milk chocolate, roughly chopped
90 ml cream
10 grams hazelnut powder
1 cup hazelnuts, finely chopped

---

1. Place the milk chocolate in a glass bowl and melt it in a microwave. You can also place the bowl over a pan of simmering water to melt – never heat chocolate over a direct flame or it will burn. Keep the melted chocolate aside.
2. Heat the cream for 2 minutes in a microwave or boil it on a medium heat.
3. Add it to the melted milk chocolate and whisk together until combined.
4. Add the hazelnut powder to the chocolate and cream and mix well.
5. Cool the chocolate mixture and refrigerate it for at least 4 hours or overnight.
6. Toast your chopped hazelnuts in a pan with no oil over a medium flame until they are browned.
7. Remove the chocolate from the fridge. The mixture should be firm but malleable at this point.
8. Using a tablespoon, scoop the chocolate into your palm and roll in only one direction to make small balls. Be careful that your palms are not too hot or the chocolate will start to melt. A bowl of ice water should be enough to help you keep your hands cool.
9. Refrigerate the truffles until they are firm and then roll them in the chopped hazelnuts until they are evenly coated.
10. Refrigerate for 20 minutes and serve on a pretty plate.

PEANUT BUTTER COOKIES

Brown sugar and chunky peanut butter come together to flavour these cookies with a warm, nutty aroma. Serve them straight out of the oven with a glass of cold milk.

SERVES 4

125	grams all-purpose flour
75	grams butter, at room temperature
115	grams brown sugar
75	grams chunky peanut butter
1	egg
½	teaspoon baking powder

Preheat your oven to 165°C

1. Using a hand mixer or a stand mixer, whisk the butter, brown sugar and peanut butter together in a bowl till soft.
2. Add the egg and whisk till properly combined.
3. Sift the flour and baking powder together in a separate bowl to evenly distribute the baking powder.
4. Slowly add the flour to your batter, using a spatula to fold it in.
5. Line a baking tray with parchment paper.
6. With a tablespoon, scoop the dough on to the baking tray in medium-sized rounds, leaving a 2-inch gap between each cookie.
7. Bake for 15 minutes or till the edges start browning.

STRAWBERRY CHEESECAKE

There's nothing quite like a really good velvety cheesecake topped with fresh seasonal fruit. Each forkful is dense, rich and light at the same time, with a hint of your childhood memories wafting through the fruit.

SERVES 4

FOR THE CRUST

200 grams digestive biscuits
50 grams butter
50 grams castor sugar

FOR THE FILLING

200 grams Philadelphia cream cheese
200 grams condensed milk
½ cup whipping cream
1 tablespoon lemon juice
15 grams gelatin
¼ cup water

Fresh strawberries, thinly sliced

Preheat your oven to 165°C

Butter and flour a 9-inch springform cake tin with a removable base.

1. Put the digestive biscuits into a Ziplock bag and seal. Grind them into fine crumbs using a rolling pin or by simply smashing them against the counter repeatedly. You may also use a food processor.
2. Melt butter in a saucepan and mix with the digestive biscuit crumb and castor sugar. The biscuits should now look and feel like wet sand.
3. Place the biscuit mixture in the cake tin and spread it over the base and up the sides, using the back of a spoon to achieve an even thickness.
4. Bake the base for 5 to 7 minutes and then leave aside to cool.
5. For the filling, whisk your cream cheese and condensed milk together in a blender.
6. Mix the gelatin with water and heat on a low flame, stirring continuously until it dissolves completely. Allow it to cool and strain it through a sieve to remove any lumps that may have remained.
7. Beat the whipping cream until thick and add it to the cream cheese mixture. Fold in the lemon juice.
8. Add the cooled gelatin in a thin stream to the mix, making sure to whisk well so there are no lumps.
9. Pour the filling carefully over the baked base. Cover and chill the cheesecake in the fridge for at least 4 to 6 hours.
10. When you are ready to serve, unmould the cheesecake carefully and place it on a flat serving dish. Decorate the top of the cheesecake with sliced strawberries and a sprig of mint for a bit of whimsy.

You may also use sliced mangoes, cherries or blueberries based on the season.

BASIC STOCK AND SAUCES

Most recipes make use of basic stock and sauces to add plenty of punch to the final dish. Whether it's infused oil, a stock or an emulsification of different ingredients, no dish would be complete without it.

VEGETABLE STOCK

2 onions, rough chopped
1 carrot, rough chopped
2 stalks celery, rough chopped
1 leek, sliced
1.5 litres water

Put all your ingredients into a deep heavy-bottomed pan with a covered lid and bring them to the boil. Allow them to cook together for 1 hour before straining the stock. Discard the solid vegetables.

FISH STOCK

1 carrot, rough chopped
1 stalk celery, rough chopped
1 white onion, rough chopped
1 pod garlic
A bay leaf
A handful of black peppercorns
Fish bones, fish heads, fish shells
2 litres water

Put all your ingredients into a deep heavy-bottomed pan and allow them to cook for 20 minutes on a gentle simmer. It should not boil or cook for longer because the stock will become cloudy and the fish may disintegrate. Strain and keep the liquid.

RED WINE ROSEMARY SAUCE

15 ml red wine reduction
15 ml balsamic vinegar reduction
20 ml strong stock
10 ml oil
1 teaspoon sugar
1 teaspoon salt
1 sprig rosemary
A handful of black pepper

Add 10 grams sugar to 100 ml of red wine and allow it to reduce on a low flame. This will give you 50 ml of reduction. You can repeat the same process for the balsamic vinegar reduction. Once you have both, mix together with the rosemary, stock, sugar and oil. Season with salt and pepper to taste.

TOMATO CONCASSE

3 medium tomatoes
A handful of basil leaves
Salt and pepper to taste

Blanche 3 medium sized tomatoes for 1 minute in boiling hot water. Skin the tomatoes and deseed. Put into blender with a handful of basil, salt and pepper. Blend until smooth.

TOMATO RELISH

1 cup tomato concasse
1 teaspoon paprika
1 teaspoon sugar
1 teaspoon apple cider vinegar
Salt and pepper to taste
A handful of fresh coriander leaves

Heat the tomato concasse at boiling point for 3 minutes, and add the paprika, salt, pepper, sugar, fresh coriander and apple cider vinegar. Stir quickly and take off the heat. Allow the mixture to cool before using it.

PIRI PIRI SAUCE

2 tablespoons lemon juice
2½ tablespoons olive oil
40 ml vinegar
1 cup yogurt
½ tablespoon cayenne pepper
½ tablespoon garlic, minced
½ tablespoon paprika
½ tablespoon salt
½ tablespoon chilli flakes

Make the piri piri sauce by blending the lemon juice, olive oil, vinegar, cayenne pepper, minced garlic, paprika, salt and chilli flakes together. Keep aside.

HARISSA MAYONNAISE

12 dry red chillis
4 cloves garlic
1 tablespoon caraway seeds
4 stems parsley
1 handful of fresh mint leaves
Lime juice to taste
Extra virgin olive oil to taste
1 cup mayonnaise

Blend all the ingredients except mayonnaise until you have a smooth paste. In another bowl, add 1 tablespoon of mayonnaise to 2 tablespoons Harissa paste and mix. Continue mixing the mayonnaise and Harissa in a 1:2 ratio until you have enough.

RUM RAISIN MUSTARD

1 cup yellow mustard
1 cup dark rum
¾ cup water
¾ cup white vinegar
½ cup honey
¼ cup white raisins
A pinch of salt

Whisk all your ingredients together in a bowl. Store in an airtight container and refrigerate until needed.

SPICY REMOULADE

¼ cup celery, chopped
10 grams parsley, chopped
10 grams gherkins
¼ cup mayonnaise

Mix together in a small bowl and refrigerate until needed.

BHUT JOLOKIA MAYONNAISE

3 tablespoons mayonnaise
1 tablespoon bhut jolokia sauce

Mix together in a small bowl and refrigerate until needed.

DILL MASCARPONE

1 cup mascarpone cream
2 tablespoons dill, chopped
1 sprig dill

Combine ingredients and mix well.

RED BELL PEPPER GEL

700 grams red bell pepper juice
100 grams water
8 grams agar agar

In a saucepan, reduce red the bell pepper juice to half its weight (this should yield 350 grams). In another pan, add water and warm. Add the agar agar and keep whisking till the gel clears. Add the bell pepper reduction and bring to a boil, whisking occasionally. Strain and refrigerate. The mixture should set into a hard, brittle gel. Cut the gel into cubes and blend once again into a smooth gel. Strain and put into a piping bag. Keep refrigerated until further use.

CONVERSIONS AND COOKING TIMES

1 tablespoon	3 teaspoons
1/16 cup	1 tablespoon
1/8 cup	2 tablespoons
1/6 cup	2 tablespoons + 2 teaspoons
1/4 cup	4 tablespoons
1/3 cup	5 tablespoons + 1 teaspoon
1/2 cup	8 tablespoons
2/3 cup	10 tablespoons + 2 teaspoons
3/4 cup	12 tablespoons
1 cup	16 tablespoons or 48 teaspoons
1 pint	2 cups
1 quart	2 pints or 4 cups
1 cup	250 ml
1 tablespoon	15 ml
1 teaspoon	5 ml

°F	°C
475	250
425	220
392	200
350	175
325	160
300	150
250	120

100 grams

100 grams water = 1/2 cup
100 grams oil = 1/2 cup

Flour = just under 1 cup
Sugar = 1/3 cup
Icing sugar = 1/3 cup + 2 tablespoons
Castor sugar = 1/3 cup + 2 tablespoons
Potato = 2 small potatoes
Red pepper = 1 medium size pepper
Yellow pepper = 1 medium size pepper
Onion = 3 small onions
Carrot = 2 medium size carrots

10 grams

Ginger = a thumb-sized piece
Garlic = 4 big cloves
Lime juice = 1/2 a lime or 3/4 tablespoon
Cornflour = 3/4 tablespoon

A GLOSSARY OF COOKING TERMS

We often find culinary terms confusing; we're sometimes unsure about what a word actually means and the method it implies but may not have someone to ask. This glossary explains the processes behind simple cooking terms that every home chef must know.

"Standing back and staring blankly at the glass, he realised he had no idea what it meant to preheat. Obviously he heated it prior to something, but to what?" ***- Ais, Evenfall***

Al dente – to cook pasta and rice 'firm to the bite', an Italian term.

Brown – to pan fry in very hot fat in order to colour the surface, usually of meat.

Braise – to cook gently in a sealed pot with stock or thick sauce.

Blanch – to cook briefly in boiling water. This is followed by plunging straight into ice-cold water to stop further cooking.

Caramelise – to cook until golden. This refers to the point where natural sugars in the food begin to turn into caramel.

Chantilly – to whip cream and sugar together, a classic French preparation.

Coat – to cover a dish with a substance, such as a sauce. This is either brushed or spooned on.

Cream – to beat eggs or butter and sugar together with a whisk or wooden spoon until they become thick and pale in colour. The colour lightens from a dark yellow to a pale yellow.

Drain – to remove the liquid from a food, usually by tipping into a sieve or colander.

Drizzle – to pour a small amount of liquid over a surface.

Dry roast – to cook in an oven without the addition of any liquid or fat.

Emulsify – to mix liquids of different densities to form a thicker liquid, commonly used when making sauces like mayonnaise.

Fold – to mix food gently from the bottom of a bowl to the top. A large metal spoon or spatula is used to lift (fold) what is at the bottom of the bowl to the top.

Gut – to remove the entrails of fish.

Julienne – to cut food into long thin strips, similar to matchsticks.

Marinate – to place raw meat or other foods in a liquid that has been flavoured with spices and aromatics prior to cooking. Marination is done anywhere between 30 minutes and a day prior to cooking to allow the meat to tenderise and absorb extra flavour.

Poach – to cook gently in barely simmering liquid, such as water, stock, or milk.

Process – to mix thoroughly with a blender or electric mixer.

Purée – to create a smooth paste from ingredients placed in a food processor or blender.

Reduce – to boil or simmer a liquid in order to evaporate water, thereby concentrating the flavour and thickening it.

Simmer – to cook slowly over a gentle heat, before the liquid comes to a boil.

Skim – to remove the frothy scum – skim – from the surface of a liquid by using a slotted spoon.

Steam – to cook in a deep pan set over boiling water with a perforated rack placed inside and a tight-fitting lid.

Thicken – to add ingredients to a sauce or soup to make it thicker, usually egg yolks or flour.

Trim – to remove the fatty or inedible parts from food, usually a piece of meat or leafy vegetables.

Whisk – to beat rapidly with a flexible tool usually known as a whisk in order to increase the volume and aerate the ingredients of the dish you are cooking.

A GLOSSARY OF INGREDIENTS

Living in India, we tend to use a lot of words interchangeably. Language becomes a meld of English, Hindi and regional dialects that is considered the daily norm. This list has been compiled to help clarify ingredients that may have an alternative name to the ones that you are used to. It is by no means conclusive and continues to grow with every day that we spend in a kitchen.

"No one who cooks, cooks alone. Even at her most solitary, a cook in the kitchen is surrounded by generations of cooks past, the advice and menus of cooks present, the wisdom of cookbook writers." - ***Laurie Colwin***

Adu-Lasan	Ginger-Garlic Paste
Almonds	Badam
Aniseed	Sauf
Asafoetida	Hing
Apricots	Jurdaloo
Bengal Gram Flour	Besan
Black-eyed Beans	Chora
Black Pepper	Kala Miri
Cardamom	Elaichi
Carom / Omum Seeds	Ajwain / Ajmo
Cashew nuts	Kaju
Cherangia	Charoli / Chirongji
Cinnamon	Dalchini / Tuj
Clove	Luvung
Coriander	Hara Dania / Kothmir
Coriander Seeds	Dhania
Cumin Seeds	Jeera
Curry Leaves	Curry Patta
Eggplant / Brinjal	Baingan
Fenugreek Seeds	Methi
Flaked Rice	Poha / Powva
Garlic	Lasan
Clarified Butter	Ghee
Ginger	Adrak / Adu
Green Chilli	Hara Mirch
Indian Salmon	Ravas
Jaggery	Gor / Gud
Lemon / Lime	Limboo
Lentils	Dal
Mint	Phudina
Mustard Seeds	Rai ka Dana
Nutmeg	Jaiphal
Okra	Bhindi
Papadum	Papad
Paprika	Mirchi ka Bhuka
Peanuts / Groundnuts	Moonghphali / Sing
Pomfret	Chhumno
Poppy Seeds	Khus Khus
Prawn / Shrimp	Jhinga / Kolmi / Kolambi
Red Chilli	Lal Mirch
Red Pumpkin	Bhopla / Kuddu / Koru
Saffron	Kesar
Seer	Surmai
Sesame Seeds	Til / Tul
Semolina	Rava / Sooji
Spinach	Palak
Sweet Potato / Yam	Kund / Sukarkand
Tamarind	Imli / Amli
Turmeric	Haldi
Vermicelli	Sevia / Sev
Yoghurt	Curd / Dahi

CONTRIBUTORS

Farrokh Khambatta is the owner and Executive Chef of JOSS - a restaurant that has been synonymous with the words Kala Ghoda for over 10 years. Reopened in Mumbai's Santa Cruz district, it still enjoys the patronage of its older South Mumbai customers.

Viraf Patel is Executive Chef and co-owner at one of Mumbai's most popular restaurants – CAFÉ ZOE. It has been voted Best All Day Diner, Best Debut Restaurant, Best European / Global Restaurant and is also listed in the Miele Guide to Asia's 500 Best Restaurants 2013.

Mukhtar Qureshi is the Executive Chef at NEEL, and part of the legendary Qureshi family of Lucknow. Neel has been voted Favourite North Indian People's Choice, Best Indian Noteworthy Newcomer and Best Debutante Restaurant Pan India.

Nikhil Chib is the owner and Head Chef of BUSABA, whose extensive menu includes French, Burmese, Korean, Thai and Vietnamese cuisine. He is one of the front runners of Oriental food in Mumbai.

Amol Patil is the Head Chef of KHYBER. The restaurant boasts North - West Frontier cuisine and is on the to-do list of most visiting tourists. It has been awarded a Certificate of Excellence by Trip Advisor and Best Fine Dining Restaurant on many occasions.

VICKY RATNANI is the face of the television shows 'Vicky goes Veg' and 'Vickypedia'. He has been a prominent part of Mumbai's food scene with more than 5 successful restaurant to his name.

Pooja Dhingra is Mumbai's macaron queen. She has wowed the city and won the hearts of thousands with the lip-smacking, delicious, gorgeous confectionery that comes pouring out of LE 15 PATISSERIE.

Nitin Kulkarni is the executive chef of INDIGO, one of Mumbai's first stand-alone fine dining restaurants. The restaurant combines old-world charm with eclectic European cuisine and the finest selection of wines.

Sanjana Patel is the Head Chef and Chief Innovator for LA FOLIE, an artisanal, innovative dessert café that adds inches to the waistline just by looking at the pastries. Her passion is a testimony to a 'love beyond obsession', and is reflected in all La Folie's stores.

KALA GHODA CAFÉ is an artistically minded part café, part bakery and part gallery set in an early 20th century barn. The menu is comprised of locally sourced organic ingredients wherever possible and their own blends of organic teas and coffees.

TRISHNA is the darling of Mumbai's seafood aficionados. Traditional Malvani cuisine is served and eaten at almost breakneck speed. It is practically impossible to walk in here and get a table.

CHETANA is one of Mumbai's oldest and best known vegetarian Indian restaurants. The undisputed king of the 'thali', a meal here is guaranteed to send you home for a nap – immediately!

KABOOM! is a cross between a food truck and a restaurant, serving up different kinds of cuisine every day. With a focus on locally produced, organic food it is making waves in Mumbai's culinary world.

Alex Sanchez is the Executive Chef at THE TABLE, which was voted Best Restaurant in India in 2014 and is also listed in the Miele Guide to Asia's 500 Best Restaurants 2013.

Annie Bafna is the owner of THE NUTCRACKER. Kala Ghoda's all-vegetarian café is always full of patrons eager to try Annie's scrumptious recipes.

Pankil Shah, Sumit Gambhir and Abhishek Honawar are co-owners and innovators of WOODSIDE INN and THE PANTRY. Each restaurant is distinctive in its flair and style and has made its own name in the market. Woodside Inn boasts comfort food, great cocktails and a homey pub feel, while The Pantry's menu comprises of food made from locally sourced, organic ingredients.

Irfan Pabaney and Rachel Goenka Khetarpal are partners in all things food. They are head chefs and owners of THE SASSY SPOON, one of Mumbai's edgiest, most popular restaurants, which has been voted India's Best Independent Restaurant and is also the Top Voted choice for European and Mediterranean food.

ACKNOWLEDGEMENTS

"A table is a meeting place, a gathering ground, the source of sustenance and nourishment, festivity, safety, and satisfaction. A person cooking is a person giving: even the simplest food is a gift." – Laurie Colwin

This has been a journey of learning, of going from one table to another – there are always so many people you find along the way, who leave a little bit of themselves behind to help you grow.

I would like to thank **Maneck Davar** and **Brinda Miller** of the **Kala Ghoda Association,** without whose support this book would not have come into being.

Each book has its own story, and this one started on just another day at a coffee shop with **Heeral Akhaury**'s brilliant idea. She has been invaluable in helping design and conceptualise the book.

Of course, no book comes through without a great publisher backing you. **Harsha Bhatkal** has been enthusiastic about this project from the start, as has **Swapna Shinde** of Popular Prakashan. It's gratifying to feel their excitement every time we meet.

Shiresh R Karrale's eye for detail and incredible talent has worked with **Amrita Rana**'s flares of creativity and genius to give us truly mouth-watering images and a delicious-looking book.

Amy Madon, **Kerman Madon**, **Jehangir Madon, Jimmy Avasia** and **Yasmin Mody**'s literary inclinations and sharp eyes have helped shape this book, as has **Fram Mody**, who is almost a co-editor and my most willing taster.

There are many others from within the Association who have contributed in different ways – my partner in all things food and co-curator of the food section **Roxanne Bamboat** as well as **Varsha Karrale**, **Kayomi Engineer, Asad Laljee**, **Aahana Miller**, **Rhea Bhambhani** and **Dhvani Mehta**.

On behalf of the Kala Ghoda Association, I would like to thank our partners **Hindustan Times** for believing in this book as well as the chefs and restaurants that have participated in the Kala Ghoda Arts Festival with unflailing enthusiasm and great support from the first year of the food vertical itself.

We would not have come this far without you.

Thank you.

Aashiyana Shroff
Abhishek Honawar
Alex Sanchez
Amal Farooqi
Amrita Rana
Annie Bafna
Arpana Gvalani
Asha Khatau
Ayushi Shah
Bongo Bong
Burma Burma
Chetana
Curtis Pintye
Dan Alluf
Degustibus Foods
De Tales
Farhad Bomanjee
Farrokh Khambatta
Gauri Devidayal
Gauri Rane Shetty
Gourmet West
Gresham Fernandes
Hopping Chef
Irfan Pabaney
Irish House
Jaydeep Mukherjee
Khyber
Le Pain Quotidien
Lemon Leaf
Masala Library
Maya Dastoor
Milind Sovani
Moshe Shek
Mukhtar Qureshi
Nevil Timbadia
Nikhil Agarwal
Nikhil Chib
Nitin Kulkarni
Padmanabh Thombre
Pallavi Sahney Sharma
Pankil Shah
Paresh Chhabria
Parthesh Patel
Parvez Shaikh
Perinaz Bhada-Tata
Perzen Patel
Pooja Dhingra
Prakash Thadani
Pratap Karunakar
Rachel Goenka Khetarpal
Radhika's Fine Teas
Rahul Akerkar
Rishad Nathani
Ruben Borah
Sahil Timbadia
Sanjana Patel
Serafina
Shilpa Sinha
Shraddha Bhurat
Snigdha Manchanda
Spenta Multimedia Pvt Ltd
Sumit Gambhir
Terttulia
The Consul General of Canada
The Food Bloggers Association of India
The Consulate of Israel
Thomas Zacharias
Tripti Bhatia
Trishna
Vicky Ratnani
Vikas Seth
Viraf Patel
Westside
Yogita Iyer
Yohaan Dattoobhai
Zeba Kohli